Dream MECHANICS

A Practical Guide to Creating Your Reality

John Moreschi Jr.

BALBOA.PRESS
A DIVISION OF HAY HOUSE

Balboa Press books may be ordered through booksellers or by contacting:

Balboa Press
A Division of Hay House
1663 Liberty Drive
Bloomington, IN 47403
www.balboapress.com
844-682-1282

Print information available on the last page.

Library of Congress Control Number: 2017900293

ISBN: 978-1-5043-7300-5 (sc)
ISBN: 978-1-5043-7301-2 (hc)
ISBN: 978-1-5043-7302-9 (e)

Balboa Press rev. date: 04/20/2021

This book is dedicated to us: The wanderers, the pioneers, the rebels, the dreamers, and the trailblazers. Those who change the world through optimism. Those who have the courage to overcome challenges, spread the light, and fulfill their destiny.

My intention for this book is to reach the hands of millions of individuals from all walks of life, on all levels of learning, both young and old who wish to consciously discover the journey. This book is a self-empowering resource for those who are determined to alter their present circumstances.

Dream Big!

Special thanks: Carl Benza, my sister Laurie Bay, Nova Soto, Rob Fournier, Candace Stuart-Findlay, Vilma Galindo, Yoli Acevedo, Miguel Ruiz, the Dooley Brothers, Dhammadipa Sak, Sagarananda Tien, Mallku Aribalo, Subodha Kerawalapitiye, Temple of Enlightenment, New York City Rescue Mission, Yonkers Public School District, University of Nevada Las Vegas, St. John's University, my dog Vito, and all of the amazing individuals I have encountered along the way ☺

Foreword

In reading this book, you are about to embark upon a wondrous journey of self-discovery and empowerment!

I first met John Moreschi Jr. in 2010. He was one of my fellow travelers exploring the mystic and beauty of Egypt with Mike Dooley's TUT group tour. We deeply connected the third day of our ten-day journey, and the magic began!

I actually first met John in a vision dream I had early in 2009, although at the time I had no clue who he was. While John helped me navigate a treacherous sandy path, as we carefully climbed up to an isolated temple high upon a hill overlooking the Nile, suddenly like a thunderbolt, the vision dream flooded back into my awareness! I realized that the dark-haired man of my vision dream was my Spirit Brother, John Moreschi Jr.!

Since that shared life-changing experience in Egypt, John has traveled all over the world visiting power centers and sacred sites on every continent. It is through his journeys and spirit quest experiences that John has recognized certain patterns and threads that interweave in support of self-realization.

Referring to these as Epiphanies, John has simplified and condensed his treasures of awareness, discovered through his own reawakening experience, and presents them in his book, Dream Mechanics: A Practical Guide to Creating Your Reality.

May you soar with expanded self-awareness knowing the Co-Creator that you are!

In Light and Gratitude,

Candace Stuart-Findlay
Transformation Facilitator / Founder
Empowered Whole Being Foundation
Author, *Spiritual Transformation Simplified™: The Six Fundamentals for Life Mastery*

Epiphanies

Epiphany – a sudden manifestation or a perception of the essential meaning of something. An intuitive grasp of reality and an illuminating discovery. (Merriam Webster 3a)

Epiphany #1

AWAKE

There comes a moment in every person's life when they reach a crossroads. That juncture can come in the form of a life altering event, a sudden break-through, an accident, a relationship, a death, or perhaps even an epiphany.

Awakening to your life's purpose is something that can happen to anyone. Far too often, people live an entire life-time and never truly awake. They carry on with themselves, a marriage, a family, and even a career with a blindfold over their eyes. To truly see is to remove the blindfold, and understand the illusion. Some spiritual circles call this Maya, or the production of illusions.

When we awake, we stop sleeping, and we arise from a sleep-like state of existence to the reality that awaits us. The Toltec wisdom says, "You can awake within the dream." This means that you come to the realization, in a sense, that we are all dreaming, and you are provided the knowledge that we can co-create the reality in which we live. We learn that life is simply a dream. And, it is at this point, that your existence is never quite the same.

Awakening is a blessing. It is a privilege to become conscious of your reality. For when you do, you can lead life in a very different manner. Life becomes a magical ride, rather than something happening to you. You will virtually live the dream of your choosing. And, by consciously living your dream, your visions and passions converge to become your reality.

When you have new eyes to see, the world becomes your playground, and you become the innocent child you once were. Exploration, curiosity, excitement, and laughter are around every corner. You are limitless in doing and having whatever your heart desires. The imagination becomes a powerful tool once again. You can use your imagination to visualize the life you wish to manifest, and direct the dream the way you wish to see it. Hence, reality becomes a projection of your thoughts, and creation is in your hands.

You can create your reality by awakening to the idea that it is, and always was, yours to create in the first place. You may have lost sight of that when you were conditioned as a child, and moved into adulthood. Now, the blindfold is off, and the journey will truly begin for you. You will move away from going through the motions of life, and into the idea that life is one big, creative masterpiece.

Individuals you meet on your journey will present themselves to you, and you will be able to see who is awake, and why they've come into your life. You will have the intuition of recognizing fellow awakened ones. And, you will be able to identify those who are on the cusp of awakening. These individuals will be drawn to your ideas and outlook. They will come to you with questions about life. They will admire your ability to stay poised and grounded during times of chaos and uncertainty. It will become your duty to guide them, educate them, and help them on their path.

The greatest thing you can do for yourself, your loved ones, and those around you is to awake and follow your dreams. Andrea Bolder said, "You must be willing to let go of who you have been to become who you were meant to be." These words resonate in a deep, substantiated manner. Awakenings occur when we are ready to relinquish who we are, and follow a path to who we wish to be. You could say that, spiritually, we embark on the journey. Our perception changes, and something happens to the way we view the world. We shift into a higher level of consciousness embracing love and peace. We begin to have a knowing that there is more to what we see every day.

At our inner most core dwells the true meaning of this dynamic life we are so blessed to lead. Tapping into this realization is a testimony to our individual awakening. Awakened people have a certain sense of light which illuminates from them. The light is the moniker of an awakened person. They carry it with them where ever they go. You may ask, how does awakening help me create my reality? The answer is simple. In an awakened state, you can intentionally create your reality. Your dreams can be joined with your current state of existence. They can merge into one. You will begin to live in a fearless manner knowing that it's all an illusion.

When we have amazing dreams we are delighted at what is happening. Your awakened life will take on the same precipice. Everything that is happening to you, and around you, will feel wonderful. It is important to understand that your life conditioning carries with it the challenges and traumas of not only you, but your parents and other loved ones as well. An awakened person realizes this, and begins to do the work necessary for self-realization.

How can that be with all the despair in the world? The moment you awaken to the idea that you are a vessel to spread love and compassion is the time that the world itself will move into better conditions. It begins with you. Many people wonder what factors help facilitate a person to awake.

In my research, Dr. Hora mentions, "Wisdom or suffering are the causes for awakening. We can be drawn by wisdom or driven by suffering." This is important because we awake due to a desire for knowledge and understanding. But, we can also awake from a prolonged period of pain and suffering. Dr. Hora goes on to say, "Suffering is the stimulus motivating us to seek solutions to the problems that grieve us." If you find yourself reading this book, more than likely, you desire change or an alternative view on how to live life. The ideas presented in this book will kick-start that new life experience.

Awakening is only the beginning. There is an impartial judgement on how one awakes, just so long as one awakes! In your awakened state, your view of life will forever be altered. It will no longer feel like a struggle, but more like a timeless quest. A sense of euphoria will be present because you will move to an elevated level of consciousness. You will look different, you will behave differently, and your reality will be enhanced. When you awaken, your life traumas will begin to heal. Your ability to be calm will improve. Your happiness will increase.

To awaken is to rebel against what we have been taught, and forge a new personal experience. An awakened person understands the importance of well-being, and begins to self-improve. With positive thoughts, we start to focus on personal growth, and do what is necessary to transform our past circumstances. Health and mental stability become priority number one. The expansion of your mind will begin to take you to corridors you have never explored. You will be lead to teachers, books, websites and places that will forever advance your consciousness. This expansion is your rite of passage into a new reality. Your awareness will amplify, and your eyes will fully open. In this awakened state, the entire life experience becomes a spiritual journey, and all roads lead us to our destiny.

Epiphany #2

RECONDITION

The moment we accept that life is a journey, and not a struggle, is the point in time where we create a shift. This shift is not only for ourselves, but for the collective conscious to move into a higher state.

From the time we enter the school system as a child, we form specific habits. We are put into an environment where there are a certain set of norms that we must conform to, or we are considered different. We are taught to obey rules, walk in a straight line, raise our hand, and in some cases even wear a uniform. All of this is being done to keep us in the mindset of imprisonment. The prison mindset is something that I believe is part of our conditioning. We are conditioned to be slaves. Our freedom is taken from us, and it only progresses as we move through the system.

Reconditioning begins with the realization that most of what we have been taught must be undone. I'm talking about the stuff that is deeply embedded into our neuroses. We must re-train or re-wire our minds to behave in a healthier manner. In doing so, our mind will open, and our horizons will expand. The choices we make will be in our best interests rather than coming from a place of inhibition. When we recondition ourselves, we naturally move into a more ethical way of being. Essentially, we restore ourselves to a good working condition. This means that we slowly deteriorate as we move through life if we aren't equipped with a mindset that teaches us otherwise.

Learn to unlearn. It is a skill that most individuals would do well to master. There is a defining moment when we understand that some of the ways we have been brought up were not necessarily in our best interests. At that point in time, the metaphorical light bulb in our mind flickers on. That is when the readjustment or recalibration of life can take place.

Our parents, siblings, grandparents, friends, teachers, and mentors come into in our world for a reason, but it does not mean they are moving through life in a way that is correct. Think about it, from the time we are children, most of us emulate others. We are raised in a "do as I do" environment. Some of us are taught to act or behave a certain way. Acting, in itself, must be something we recondition ourselves to undo. We are not on a stage. The more we emulate others, the more we move from our authentic selves. We slowly lose our own sense of who we are. Creativity becomes less and less, and the ability to use our minds becomes stagnant. We become conditioned to be more like robots rather than happy, conscious, and creative individuals.

In order to repair ourselves, we must recognize that we have been placed into a very specific design. We learn to separate ourselves from the status quo. A reconditioned individual understands their current state of affairs, and then takes the necessary steps to improve their situation. Reconditioning returns us to a better functioning state.

The idea that we are a part of a whole is a holistic concept that we begin to grasp. Holistic or organic living aligns with reconditioning. As we move from an individual, materialistic mindset to a collective, empathetic mindset, our world will inevitably change for the better.

One of the greatest authors on the planet, Paolo Coelho, said, "The universe conspires in our favor." This simple quote has the power to change lives. Everything that is happening to or around us is for our own benefit. I remember the first time I read that quote. I was going through a reconditioning period in my own life. This quote captured me in so many ways. It basically re-wired my thinking because no matter what conditions we are presented with, or how devastating a situation may be, it is safe knowing that it's happening for our best interests. The universe is a precise and intricate place. It is all-knowing and works in ways that are beyond our comprehension. To work with this knowledge is to begin to live the dream. Creating your reality will be easier knowing that the universe is working in your favor. The choices you make will be made having this knowledge in mind.

Reconditioning does take time and practice just like anything you want to get good at. Currently, you have an entire life of conditioning in your mind. And, your environment or the neighborhood you live in may be just as conditioned. It will take time to readjust the things going on in your mind. But, this whole idea of creating your reality is an inside job. Once you start repairing yourself internally, your entire external experience will change.

You can begin by putting positive thoughts, and images in your mind. This is a simple practice that helps tremendously. Surround yourself with others who think on this level. Read books that are designed to improve yourself. Do activities that are beautiful.

Volunteer yourself, and your time, to help those in need. Open your heart.

Everything you do in this universe comes back to you. It may come back in a different form than how you gave it, but it does come back. We live in a world of duality. Understanding the nature of this duality will help you in your life experience. Therefore, not every experience has to be good or bad. It can just be an experience without the emotional charge behind it.

Reconditioning is a system overhaul. It is restoring something to good condition or working order. And, in this case, that something is your mind. When you recondition this vital component of your operating system, the rest of your system will operate better. The best part of reconditioning is you are the same person, but your perception is revamped.

Reconditioning is a fascinating process. It allows you to examine yourself, and make the changes that are necessary to live the life of your dreams. If you had the tools to do this, wouldn't you begin working on it right away? There are specific tools being presented to you here in this book. Use them.

Your performance will improve as you re-wire your thinking to help you bring about better circumstances on your journey. We can recapture the innocence and creativity of our youth when we become cognizant of how our minds work. Our brain is built to heal and rejuvenate itself. So pay no mind to your current circumstances, deep-rooted conditioning, and negative thought patterns that you may have developed. They can all be transformed.

Re-envision your life, and then begin to align yourself with ideas that will seed your sub-conscious. Be specific and clear on what your life should look like so it may grow in that direction. Practice this technique daily, and your reality will begin to change. Focus your energy on what it is that you wish to create, not on what is troubling you. And, if you find yourself hesitating on certain decisions, then look at that as a signal that you may want to go in another direction.

Your feelings will help guide you when you recondition yourself to trust them. Some people refer to the mechanism called your gut. I like to refer to this as intuition. Either way, we have a stored memory of our subconscious experiences that we can call upon. Our intuition catalogs through our stored memories to help us make better decisions. We aren't taught in school systems to follow these important insights. When we recondition ourselves to utilize instincts and intuition, we can call upon them to help create a more favorable reality.

As we grow spiritually, we revise our beliefs and understanding with new knowledge. In some respect, the expansion of knowledge requires us to continually recondition our minds. In order to create new experiences, we have to dismantle older knowledge so we may broaden our capacity to co-create. In many respects, when we expand our consciousness, the former self will begin to fall away so the higher self can emerge.

Epiphany #3

MANIFESTATION

"Everything in your life is a manifestation of your imagination, you're making it up as you go along (Livin3.com)."

What exactly is manifestation? According to the Free Dictionary, "Manifestation is the indication of the existence or reality of something." It is an outward expression. Simply stated, manifestation is an inner thought that appears on the physical plane. It is the idea that something can be created externally, even though the concept actually began internally.

From a spiritual perspective, manifestation is where the unseen becomes seen. It is the place where the vision becomes the reality, or the non-existent becomes existent. Individuals like Walt Disney called it imagination. Whatever we can conceive in our minds, can and does become real with a prolonged period of attention on those thoughts.

We can achieve so many things with manifestation. Manifestation is a profound, life-altering technique, that when mastered, can serve us in many ways. We can tap into the art of manifestation for health, travel, money, career…you name it! The beauty about manifestation is that it can be a tool to help us create our reality. This book is a result of manifestation. It started as an intention or an inward vision. With prolonged thought, the book has appeared on the physical plane.

In order to manifest, it is a good idea to have thoughts about what it is you wish to create, but it's an even better idea to write down all the reasons WHY you want to create it. For example, this book was intended to reach individuals on many levels. It was designed to share knowledge. The book is a free expression of the thoughts that go into the art of manifesting. All of the ideas for its contents were internal at one point, then they were written down to see on a daily basis. Now, here in your hands or on your digital device that book has come to be.

If you look all around you, everything that has come into existence was first a thought in someone's mind. A car, a home, a piece of clothing, and even a person. Through persistent thought and intention, things will manifest. Manifestation is one of the greatest steps in the creation process. It is essential to learn how it works in order to create the reality you desire. By invoking manifestation, you can create the life of your dreams.

Manifestation is at the core of Dream Mechanics, and a vital resource one can learn. You can easily manifest through affirmation, visualization, or thought invocation. When implemented properly, manifestation will become your new best friend. The trick to manifestation is belief and feeling.

Andy Dooley proclaimed, "Feeling first…manifestation second." You have to truly believe you can achieve something in order to achieve it. You also want to surround that same belief with as much emotional energy as possible. Feel how happy you will be when the thing you want, or situation you wish for, becomes reality. When we do this, manifestation will start to become second nature, and the process will accelerate.

The sub-conscious, by definition, "Is the part of the mind which one is not fully aware, but influences one's actions and feelings." You have to feed that sub-conscious with visualizations and images that will influence your manifestations. Some of us do this through meditation. During meditation we see things by going deep into our sub-conscious. We feel what love and happiness feels like.

Others manifest through art. These individuals paint what it is they wish to see in their reality before it actually happens. For example, I did this with the infamous Northern Lights. I painted an image of a place in Alaska complete with snow and evergreen trees. I painted beautiful colors in the night sky such as greens, purples, and blues. I'll have you know, about a six months after I completed that painting, I took a trip to Fairbanks, Alaska. One night during the trip, I was in a room with some individuals who were up late waiting to catch a glimpse of the Northern Lights. As the night sky began to twirl with color, we hurried outside to see the lights. I didn't bring any fancy camera equipment, so I asked a photographer if he would take my picture. I received an email from that photographer about three weeks later. The picture he took of me looked almost identical to the painting of the Northern Lights I painted six months prior to that trip. Manifestation is real!

Visualization through any means is transcending. It is a proven way to create your reality. The only advice I would impart is to allow time for the manifestations of what you visualize to occur. The universe will co-create with your pre-meditated visualizations and thoughts. Sometimes, manifestations happen quickly, and other times they pop-up when you least expect them. They do arrive, and when they do, be prepared to recognize them so you can manifest even more.

Right now, most of us are actually manifesting on auto-pilot. Basically, we don't even know that we are doing it. We can manifest either negatively or positively. Imagine if you could manifest at will, and direct those manifestations to live the life of your dreams. Being conscious of manifestation can be revolutionary for an individual, and their entire life experience.

Our word and how we direct our speech has an impact on manifestation as well. The energy you put into the world comes from your language and thoughts. Be aware of how you speak to others, the tone you use, and the vibration you emit. All of these have a direct impact on your manifestations. They are components of the manifestation process. In order to bring your manifestations onto the physical plane, we also have to pay attention that our actions and behavior match what it is we wish to manifest.

Manifestation is an acquired skill for creating your reality. There are numerous books and techniques that are available on the subject of manifesting. In addition, affirmations are a powerful tool to assist in the manifestation process. An affirmation is the assertion that something exists, or is true, until it literally becomes real. For example, "I am happy, healthy, and prosperous." Repeatedly saying these words will bring them into your experience. Speaking affirmations aloud or writing them down, where you can see them daily, is a super conductor for manifesting. The energy that you place in your affirmation is directly linked to your manifestation. Utilize affirmations to increase your success of manifesting, and create the life you've always dreamed of!

$$E = mc^2$$

Epiphany #4

FORMULA

There is a formula for co-creating our reality. It is as simple as this:

- **S**et an intention.
- **I**magine what you want.
- **F**ollow-up with action.
- **T**rust in the process.

The acronym for this method is SIFT. By following the steps in this formula, you will sift through a myriad of your thoughts. It will help you create your reality by examining the thoughts that are most important and useful.

The interpretation of the formula is meant to provide a thought pattern for you to utilize. It will take practice to form this thought habit, but once you do, you can go on creating the reality you so desire. For example, if you are reading this book, you have set an intention. The intention could be wanting to alter your current circumstances, or you may wish to live the life of your dreams.

The same intent that you are using to pick up this book is the intention you require when creating your reality.

Next, imagine what it is that you want. Write these things down on a piece of paper. List all the reasons you want something so you gain the feeling of having it already.

Then, take some appropriate action toward your desire. For instance, go on the internet and start planning that dream vacation. Price out the flights and the hotels. Look at pictures of the beaches you want to see yourself lying on. Research the activities or spa treatment you want to experience.

Finally, trust in the process. Trusting in what you are doing is imperative. Trust is the cornerstone of this formula. Suzy Kassem said, "Doubt kills more dreams than failure ever will." You have to trust in what is being presented to you here, and take appropriate action to move you toward what-ever it is you wish to create. Cut out pictures, hang them on your walls, or create a vision board. Do whatever it takes to put the images of the life you want to create into your sub-conscious, and they will become your reality.

This is a tried and true, proven formula. People often wonder how individuals reach certain heights, accumulate certain things, or travel around the globe. It's really not rocket science. Any individual who has achieved anything…first had an intention. Intention is the spark of manifestation. In addition, we have an inner guidance system or compass to help guide us. Think of a GPS navigation system. All you do is type in the address you want to reach, steer the car or yourself for that matter, and follow the directions to reach your destination. It's that simple!

The SIFT formula follows the exact same premise. Know what it is you want, place in your mind the vision you wish to create, then take appropriate action, and trust you will be guided until that vision becomes real.

We are sophisticated vehicles that have many complex, intricate parts. We are designed to do amazing things. Unleashing that potential is a direct result of following a specific pattern or formula. This formula can be brought into anything that we do. The universe is designed in a precise geometric pattern with unfaltering math. That same formula works for every fabric of our lives.

Let's review another example. Many people claim they wish they had more time to do the things in life they wish to you do. This is the moment where you set *balance* as your intention. Focus on the idea that you want more time for work, family, and leisure. Hang a picture on the wall, where you can see it every day, which reads, "BALANCE." Or, write on an index card, "I have all the time in the world," and hang it on your bathroom mirror where you can see it daily. You will find that you will begin to draw into your life all the things that will help you create balance, and more time to do the things you really want to do will be yours! Perhaps you will start a meditation or yoga practice. Perhaps you will ask your employer to keep your schedule more consistent. Your freedom will open up to you. Now here's the kicker, if the route you're taking is not getting you to your destination, then it's either time to set an alternate route, or take some necessary detours to get you there. The choice is yours and entirely up to you.

Remember, all formulas contain a solution. If you can get into a solution-based mentality, your life is going to go smoother. You can co-create with the universe by following the simple steps of

SIFT. It is a simple formula that works. I thought about adding another step to this process, but it actually leads into the next epiphany. When you trust in the process you have to **let go** of all the thoughts that try to impede upon you from successfully completing the formula. Coincidentally, that brings us to our next epiphany...

Epiphany #5

LETTING GO

Steve Maraboli said, "Let today be the day you learn the grace of letting go and the power of moving on."

Letting go is one of the most challenging aspects for individuals to grasp. It could very well be the greatest obstacle of the human condition. Perhaps, it is something in our DNA which prevents us from letting go.

On a global scale, the world would be a more harmonious place if people, families, communities, nations, and government officials learn to let go. When we were children we learned the word "mine!" That is MY toy, that is MY room, and those are MY things. As a society, those are OUR borders, OUR resources, or OUR political party. Attachment to things became embedded in our psyche. A sense of entitlement influenced our minds through conditioning. Ultimately, this ideology leads to a path of division.

It is a blessing to those who taught us how to relinquish our attachments because letting go is something that doesn't come easy for many of us. How many situations have you been involved in where it was difficult to let go? How many times did you try to hold on to something that was meant to be free? Often, as children, we are taught to hold on to things. When you let go, the whole universe opens itself to you. Anything is possible at that moment. This is called, "being in the flow." When you are in the flow, life naturally carries you along. You feel weightless and light as a feather. It's like entering a running stream of water. The water doesn't struggle to flow. It just flows.

It feels good to let go. It feels good to others when we let go. Letting go is essential in opening up a space for manifestation to take place. It is one of the most powerful steps to comprehend in order to create the life you desire. When we let go of the controls, anything is possible!

When we are in a state of uncertainty, often we are told things like, "get a grip." But, when we can let go of the grip, or the fears that fester deep inside us, joy peaks it head out in an unprecedented way. Life becomes blissful. We feel better and more at ease.

The single most important part of a journey is allowing the road to simply present itself to us! If you are too busy trying to schedule, plan, and control…how can life work its magic for you? Believe me, life is a magical ride once you know how that ride operates.

Letting go is a powerful exercise in creating your reality. Let go of the drama in your life right now. Far too often, many of us are conditioned to control our life, and even the life of others. We get intertwined with the non-sense of one another's drama. It is unhealthy when we have to be in the know all the time, or continually contribute to the daily rumor mill. Be authentic, and just let things be. Live in laughter and love by being a vessel of freedom. And, allow others to do the same.

Be careful not to take the role of victim in any situation because that is where you give your freedom away. Your personal power has more strength than you think. Envision yourself in an environment where your personal power matters. Relinquish the need to orchestrate your affairs. In the spirit of letting go, "do you have the power to give power away?" This statement echoes the relevance of letting go! Try it, you'll be surprised how much it serves you, and makes you feel good in times of tension.

When we find ourselves in negative or challenging situations, the power to walk away changes our experience. Always feel good about removing yourself from anything that feels uncomfortable. This is a true expression of letting go. If you're reading this book than you have come to a juncture in your life where you wish to create change. It's ok to let go of what is no longer working for you because that's how we grow. That's how personal development and self-improvement take flight. You will receive different results in life by doing things in a manner that serves you better. Your reality will change when you choose to recognize what's going on, and do the work to improve your present circumstances.

The dream comes to those who imagine things differently, and act in accordance with those images. Our decisions and choices matter because that is where our freedom resides. Make good choices, and reap the benefits of a good life. Do the things that feel right, and see hurdles transform into opportunities. Breaking through your personal walls is the most effective medicine you can prescribe to yourself. You will heal yourself in the process, and move to greater levels of awareness. Anything that you're holding onto today, can be gone tomorrow. Let go and enjoy the wonder of life!

One of my favorite teachers, Thich Nhat Hanh, said, "Letting go gives us freedom, and freedom is the condition for happiness." This is such a profound statement from an individual who is a leading peace activist. Part of Dream Mechanics, and creating your reality, is being happy throughout the process. The simple gesture of letting go provides you a vehicle to cruise along the highway of your dreams!

Epiphany #6

BACK TO BASICS

Kron Gracie said, "Everything in life goes back to basics."

The idea that, "less is more" has never been more prevalent than living in today's world. We are so materially possessed, that we have forgotten the beauty of the basic tenets of life.

Going back to the basics means being mindful of how we treat the earth, how much we consume, and how we view the world we live in. Holistically, we understand that we are part of a whole. We are one unified field so to speak. Back to the basics is a philosophical approach that reminds us to think in a manner that is conducive for everyone and everything. We move away from individualism, and toward a sense of collective consciousness. The notion of separation and division vanishes. Cohesion and togetherness arises. Communities and relationships flourish when we return to the basics.

Back to the basics is having the ability to speak straightforward and to the point. Being basic allows our mind to rest. Hence, we can become clear in our decision making process, and feel more refreshed without the burdens of everyday life. How often in your journey have you heard the saying, "keep it simple?" These words are often overlooked, but have a way of re-surfacing at various points in life. By moving away from a drama-filled, complicated life, we learn to breathe and live with ease.

Think about many of our elders. They come to a realization that life should be kept simple in their final years. It's odd that we accept this mindset when we know that life is coming to a close. Imagine if we embraced that ideology in earlier stages of life. We would have more enjoyment, peace, and satisfaction with a back to the basics approach. Health and spirituality would hold precedence over all else.

Declutter your life. Remove the things that no longer serve you, have a purpose, or function properly. Less is more because we've added so many "things" to our lives, that it effects our thoughts and decision making process. We've given ourselves a heavy burden of material possessions that have a bearing on our happiness. Lighten the load, and live a life of joyfulness!

When we return to the basics, we identify the small things that make us happy. We realize the very basic things we require to exist. We speak in very basic terms. The act of breathing becomes a treasure. Taking a long walk with a loved one, or by ourselves is healing. Sitting by a fire becomes therapeutic.

We also become aware of how much energy we are consuming. We realize that we are connected to one another and to the planet. We become more conscious of our words and actions. We are careful of how much we take, and instead find ways to give away. Back to basics returns us to what is truly necessary for contentment. We focus on the primordial elements. We become aware of our fundamental feelings before we started effecting them with more and more stuff.

Look around you right now. Look at all the things you have. The clothes, the technology, the shoes, and the furniture. What are you really using on a daily basis?

There is a movement to return to traditional living before life and society became too complicated and impulsive. There is a way to go back to the basics, and still be a contributing member of society. You will have more inner peace, more freedom, and more time to enjoy your newly created reality. Your simplified conditions will become the foundation for living your dreams. Decisions and choices will be made with ease. Solutions to everyday challenges will come naturally. Clarity will prevail over our complex minds, and the complex minds of others.

The rewards of a back to basics lifestyle are endless.

We also become more mindful of what we are eating and doing with our lives. Our mindset changes from the average person. We enjoy nature, music, art, and calm surroundings. Many of us have bought into a consumer driven and artificial lifestyle. It was part of our conditioning when we were young, and we fell for it. I'm not saying go live off the grid, and get water from a well. I'm suggesting living in a manner that connects you to the harmony of your surroundings. You will feel better if you can truly do that again.

"Going back to the basics strengthens your foundation (Iota of Truth)." If your foundation is strong, you will be able to withstand a variety of challenges as you go about deliberately creating your reality. Obstacles will easily fall away as you move closer to living the dream, and you will understand the mechanics to manifest it all!

Epiphany #7

SURRENDER

According to Webster's dictionary, "Surrender is defined as an agreement to stop fighting." Life is meant to be a magical ride, and in order to cue the magic, we must learn to surrender.

Now, that can be a challenge for many of us because we are taught to fight from the time we are pulled out of the womb. We come in kicking, screaming, and crying! All the emotions that our mother and father felt are placed into us when we are conceived.

For some of us, life seemed like a struggle right from the start. When we enter school, we are conditioned to "hit back" if someone hurts us. Parents often provide this advice to children as a means to encourage them to stick up for themselves, but when we surrender, we give up our power to something greater than ourselves. We come to the realization that life isn't a struggle.

We give up trying to control or retaliate, and we yield to an unseen force. We stop interfering with what the universe is trying to deliver to us because surrendering to the universe puts you in the flow. You enter a stream where you can be carried along effortlessly. Many religions incorporate surrendering to the will of their chosen God. Spiritually, surrender means, "a believer completely gives up his own will and subjects his thoughts, ideas, and deeds to the will and teachings of a higher power."

As we move through life, we are taught that we have to put forth effort to achieve our dreams. The process of achieving more through less effort is a new concept for many of us to absorb. Once we do, the effects are staggering.

The path of least resistance deserves to be brought to light. The path of least resistance is the physical or metaphorical pathway that provides the least effort to move forward. The concept is often used to describe why an object or entity takes a given path (Wikipedia). When we take the path of least resistance, our life experience is more pleasant and joyful. For example, when you are in a conversation or situation with someone and you feel tension, that is your mental trigger to stop, recognize what is happening, and take a less aggressive approach. In all actuality, you surrender to the situation, and an easy way will present itself to you. Resistance is often used as a metaphor for personal effort or confrontation. An individual who chooses the path of least resistance acknowledges the situation for what it is, and then elects the path that feels easiest.

Sometimes this will mean taking the road less traveled. And in doing so, you will become a pioneer in your pursuit. That is what optimists do! They pave the way for others to follow. Keep this in mind as you take the ideas presented in this book, and put them into practice. Things are going to feel different. You are going to work with these ideas, and you will find yourself in unchartered territory at times. Just remember to stay the course, remain positive, and ride the wave to create a new life for yourself. The one you've always dreamed of. Right here, right now, in this very moment.

Sonia Ricotti said, "Surrender to what is. Let go of what was, and have faith in what will be." These words are ringers of truth. They are fundamental principles that are relative to Dream Mechanics. Learn them, and then surrender to them to learn even more. Knowledge comes to those who let go of all they think they know. The open-minded reap the rewards of the unseen force that is working through all of us.

We are all one, and it is wise to simply surrender to life, and allow life to carry you along. You will find yourself in the most amazing places. You will meet the most incredible people. Your life experience will shift because you are now connected with a universal force that is precise and all-knowing. It wants what you want. It wants to give you what you wish to create. You just have to tap into it, and surrender to its power.

As a life-long student of its capabilities, I am continually surprised at what it does for me. You will be too if you allow the universe to work with you.

Epiphany #8

BALANCE

Most of us are in a hurry! Far too often I ask people how they are doing, and the response is, "I'm so busy." We are running to and fro, distracted with technology, and going from one thing to the next. We were conditioned since elementary school to be busy little bees. But, thank goodness for that age-old Aesop fable which taught us, "Slow and steady wins the race."

Learning patience is quite frankly a life-long process. But, once you have a handle on being patient, life tends to flow better. It doesn't feel forced or chaotic. With patience, we breathe easier knowing that we have all the time in the world. Patience leads to the wisdom of balance.

Many individuals try to fill their days with things to do. Some of us even have a to-do list. At one stage in my life, I lived by a to-do list. It was literally a list that I kept by my desk with all the things I had to-do. And each day I would cross things off that list as I completed them. Until, I re-learned to throw that insane, unbalancing list out the window. After that, I began to live and work more organically, and move through life naturally.

I compare a balanced way of being to nature itself. Nature doesn't struggle to grow. Nature just grows. I've used this metaphor in my life to attain more balance. When I stopped struggling with my life, it began to have wings of its' own. Patience grew through meditation. Then came harmony, and eventually more balance.

Health, work, family, travel and social time require balance. Balance creates an easiness that exudes confidence. Think of a see-saw. If one side is heavier than the other, that side goes down, and the lighter side goes up. But if each side is equally distributed, the see-saw remains even. Neither side goes up or down. In relation to life, one aspect doesn't outweigh the other, and they all get equal distribution. It is a challenge to create balance because of all the people and activities that try to grab our attention. You have to recognize when one area is getting too much of your time, and then make necessary adjustments. With these adjustments, no area consumes another.

This book will bring you balance if you apply the concepts. I observe many individuals who are literally running through life like chickens with their heads cut off. Bouncing from one thing to another. They're simply reacting to everything that is happening to them, rather than absorbing and living in the moment. This reaction breeds more reaction. Individuals and their minds are moving so rapidly that they forget to simply focus on their breath and center themselves. Before you know it, they have become bodies of impulse, and you can feel that nervous energy when you are around them or talking with them. Their life becomes a series of distractions, or they tune out completely waiting for the next impulse.

Stillness and concentration are tools that assist in developing balance. Balance allows us to cope with unexpected situations and events that may show up in our lives. Koi Fresco stated, "Balance is the key to everything. What we do, eat, think, say, feel, they all require awareness, and through this awareness we can grow."

Balance is not found, it is achieved or created.

Be conscious when one activity in your life is consuming another, and be quick to put yourself in check when it does. The reason for this suggestion is because I've been at a place where one thing in my life consumed everything else. It is vital, in the creation of reality, to check yourself throughout the process. Ask yourself, am I giving an equal amount of energy to all facets of my life? This delicate balance can mean all the difference in your manifestations and well-being.

As I mentioned, meditation and yoga are helpful resources in maintaining balance, and we will touch more on the importance of meditation later. But, this idea of balance is worthy of examination. The habitual patterns that we form take time to overcome and repair. There is a certain amount of reflection that we must do in order to create balance. Balance is an important element of Dream Mechanics. Once we achieve it, we are never quite the same again. We are better!

Epiphany #9

UNCERTAINTY

Tina Seelig said, "Uncertainty is the essence of life, and it fuels opportunity."

Entering into a situation of uncertainty can be transforming. Uncertainty means going into the unknown. It means going past our fears, and welcoming what happens next with an open mind. So many of us try to hold on to everything, plan for everything, and anticipate everything. Uncertainty reminds us that much of life is simply out of our control.

Uncertainty ties into living in the moment. Some of our most amazing experiences in life come from periods of being uncertain of what will happen next. This allows us to focus on the present moment by not moving into the past or the future. Uncertainty allows for free-flowing creativity and ideas to take form. We move into uncertainty with the understanding that the outcome will be positive regardless of what we are faced with.

How can we move forward during uncertainty? We let go and trust in the creative process of life. We hand over whatever it is that we are uncertain about, and know that our life will be altered for the better. The anxiety that comes from uncertainty can be transmuted into joy. The way we do this is by not worrying about what will happen or could happen.

We seek out unfamiliar territory because it is there that we create new and beautiful experiences. We recondition our minds not to go into a fight or flight mode in times of threat or uncertainty. We dwell on positive outcomes because we are the architects of our reality.

Our minds are so incredibly designed that they store vast amounts of memories. These memories are triggers in times of uncertainty. Those memories are often what hold us back, or propel us forward, in achieving our dreams and creating our reality. Our brain sends signals to different parts of our body when we don't know what is about to happen. It comes up with many different scenarios about what could happen in times of uncertainty.

In all reality, when we just give uncertainty a chance to play itself out, it's almost always better than we thought it would be. In fact, the majority of the time we add unnecessary fuel to the uncertainty with worry and doubt. The best way to deal with an uncertain situation is by realizing that it is a path to achieve your dreams.

Uncertainty is a disguised form of opportunity. When we master uncertainty, more of our dreams become reality. Throwing caution to the wind opens doorways. These doorways can then be walked through because they were only walls in our minds. Break through those walls, and any wall for that matter, by realizing they are only an illusion.

Uncertainty guides us to move out of our comfort zone. When we go into that space, all the wonder awaits us. It is here where we can make our dreams a reality. It is here where we can create the life we want for ourselves, not the lives we've settled for.

Today, I invite you do something you have been uncertain about. Whatever it is. Call or text a person you haven't spoken to in a while. Take a spontaneous trip. Go for a drive on a road you've never driven on. Do anything that moves you out of the place you think that you are stuck in. Do it and do it now!

Celestine Chua proclaimed, "Fear, uncertainty, and discomfort are your compasses toward growth." Shedding a positive light on the things that scare us is enlightening. Knowing how to use what we fear to our advantage is wisdom. Our inner compass provides us direction. We just have to simply trust its guidance even when it appears to be off course. Some of the best experiences are waiting to be had when we detour into uncertainty.

Thru uncertainty we become trail blazers, and reach new frontiers. We enhance our joy of living and create a new reality in the process. If happiness is what we are all after, then going into uncertainty is a means to get us there. We must not become stagnate or stranded in our quest.

Often times I hear people tell me they feel stuck by their present circumstances. They know what they should do, but they don't do it. They never get to the destination they are meant to reach. Or, they're not sure what decisions to make. Indecisiveness can easily be overcome by making little decisions that you are unsure of. To them I say, do what is easiest, do what feels good, and take a small step. Any step in the direction of your dreams is positive progression. All forward motion counts.

Our inner compass tells us what to do if we pay attention to how we feel. The compass will direct you if your feelings are in alignment with the reality you wish to create. Be a silent witness to your life. If you like what you are witnessing in your life, then your compass is functioning properly. Your priority is to recognize when things are in alignment with your dreams by being vigilant of your surroundings. Trust where your compass is leading you to reach your destiny.

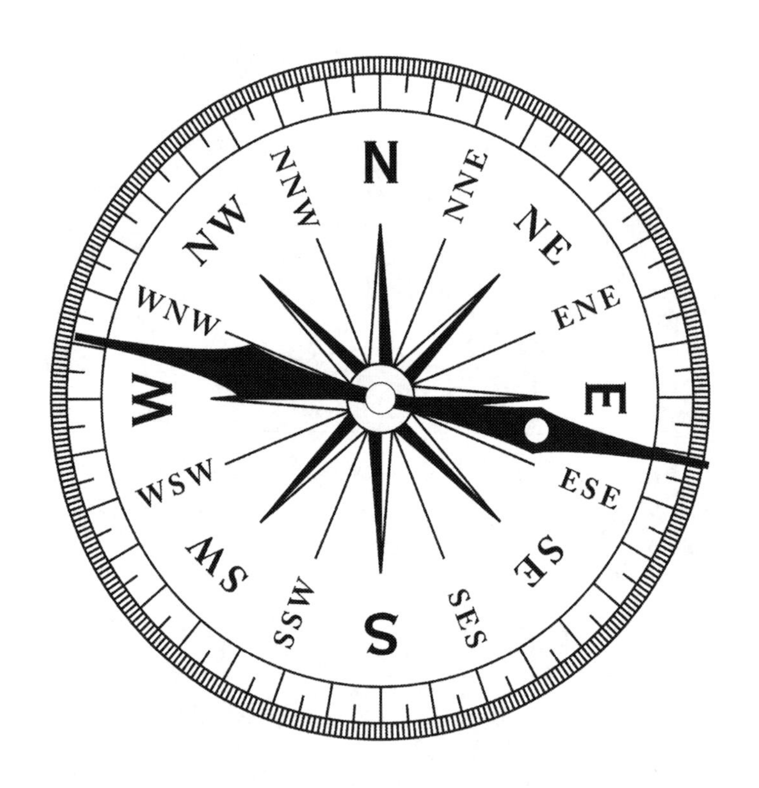
N
NNE
NE
ENE
E
ESE
SE
SES
S
SSW
SW
WSW
W
WNW
NW
NNW

Epiphany #10

LEAP OF FAITH

Margaret Shepard eloquently said, "Sometimes your only available transportation is a leap of faith."

Taking a leap of faith is no small feat for some of us. They require letting go of everything you know or think you know. Leaps of faith can be a challenge for many of us because of fear.

A leap of faith is a complete trusting of the universe or higher power to take you to a new destination. Some of us take these leaps all the time, and live a life of magic and wonder. Others, compare a leap of faith to riding a roller coaster for the first time. All the energy and emotion builds up as you wait in line. As you get closer your heart starts to beat at a rapid pace. You approach the person who ushers you to your seat. You strap in, the roller coaster begins to move, and there's no turning back now. You climb the initial hill knowing that a huge drop awaits you with several twists and turns. What do you do at that moment? You hang on and enjoy the ride!

I have to remember that some people go a whole lifetime without taking a single leap of faith. These individuals are planned, and play the game of life safely. I'm so accustomed to taking leaps of faith, that they feel less like anxiety and more like exhilaration now. Exploring our entire planet takes leap after leap after leap.

It is ok to recognize fear which may be holding you back. Fear is an intrinsic part of the human condition. It's in sharing the knowledge, that we have nothing to fear, that sets us all free. It's all in our minds and past conditioning. We put those triggers in place based upon the events and traumas we've experienced throughout our individual lives.

The good news is, we also put in place triggers of joy and happiness. If we visualize that our leaps of faith will lead us to a better experience that is exactly what we will manifest. The more we take them, the more our minds will store them as triggers for future use. Leaps of faith are required in creating the reality of your dreams. They are an essential component of Dream Mechanics.

Get out there and take a leap of faith. Do it for yourself and all the people around you. You will look different, feel different, and behave differently. You will have understood a key ingredient of those who are living the life of their dreams.

Remember, a leap of faith, coupled with trust, will magnify your manifestations. The power to manifest, when you trust in the process, is like money in the bank. Trusting, and more trusting, is like building interest and more interest. You will reap the rewards when you combine any of the epiphanies mentioned in this book with trust. Think about it...who trusts anyone these days? And, therein lies our greatest challenge. Change your thinking, and trust every single person or situation that comes into your life. Know that they are being presented to you for your well-being even if it doesn't appear to be so on the surface. Trust when things don't go the way you anticipate, the universe is revealing something even better suited for you!

If you want to live an epic life, you have to think outside the box, and get out of your comfort zone. That's where the magic is located to create your reality. Many people say, how do I get out of my comfort zone? It is very simple. If you are living the same day over and over again, congratulations you've achieved routine! Routine is great to some degree, and provides discipline. But, routine also leads to being stagnant, and joining the ranks of the status quo. Now, if you are experiencing something new on a regular basis, then you are getting out of your comfort zone. You are on your way to creating that new reality you wish to see manifest in your life.

"By leaving behind your old self and taking a leap of faith into the unknown, you find out what you are truly capable of becoming."
— Unknown.

Epiphany #11

JOY

Walter Scott poignantly stated, "Sleep in peace, and wake in joy."

Do you know what makes you happy? Have you taken the time to identify the things that make you smile? It could be an individual you know, a walk in nature, an incredible meal, or even the ability to travel freely that brings you joy. There are a variety of things that can make us feel joyful. But, are we doing these things on a daily basis? Are we intentionally setting aside the opportunity to put ourselves in situations that make us feel good?

The development of joyfulness and mirth is imperative for creating the reality we wish to manifest. Manifestation coming from a place of joy is awe inspiring. Remember, we can manifest coming from other places of emotion so be aware. That is why we must be in-tune to how we are feeling at all times.

Living in joy is a choice. Joy places you in a refined state of consciousness. You can perceive everything around you in a way that is beautiful and surreal, or you can focus on it as being something else. It is very important to understand that joy-based living produces amazing results. Think about the last time you were doing something fun, and forgot about all the things that typically go through your mind on a daily basis. The day went by so effortlessly, you lost track of time, you were absorbed in the moment, and you were smiling from ear to ear.

We can repeat these situations by checking in on ourselves. If you're feeling tired, go for a brisk walk on a sunny day. If you're feeling busy, slow down and just focus on the simple act of breathing. Most of us are moving so fast, we don't even realize we are breathing. It's unbelievable! When is the last time, you just breathed in and out for 10 seconds and focused just on that? Joyfulness is located in these simple breaths.

If you can use this ideology to catapult you to more joy, you are in for a big surprise. There is not a day that goes by, that I don't smile for a few minutes. Even if I'm by myself or in meditation, I take a moment to smile. By the way, joy is a natural anecdote for all kinds of ailments. A mind filled with joy has the ability to heal. We can listen to some lovely music, watch a two-minute comedy sketch on you-tube, or go to the beach. Cultivating joy can change the trajectory of our life. You will manifest a whole new reality when you come from a place of joy.

Throughout my journey, I've heard various sayings like, "be here now" or "you are here." What do these actually mean? I'll share with you this…joy can be found in the simplicity of the moment right where you are. And, that is very powerful to understand. We don't have to be put in places, outside of our present circumstances, to feel joy. In fact, if you can feel joy in your present state, more joy will open up to you. Perhaps joy will come outside of your present circumstances if that's what you wish to manifest. But, in order to get there, you have to start from where you are presently.

I can't tell you how many times I've heard people say, "Oh, I'll be happy when I win the lottery." What about being happy first, and then possibly winning the lottery? That is exactly what I mean about finding joy in the present moment. If you can find the joy now, then perhaps the lottery will be yours in the future. If you're buried in a cell-phone or inundated with a local drama program on television, these are not typical places of joy. They are places of pre-occupation. You may have programmed yourself to enjoy doing these things, but are they really bringing you genuine joy? I'm speaking about the joy you feel when you hear a story where someone has triumphed, or stretched beyond the norm. Or, the simple joy you feel when a person smiles at you.

Again, it is important to craft situations for yourself that provide joy. Joyful feelings are treasures for the mind, body, and soul. Eckhart Tolle wrote, "Pleasure is always derived from something outside you, whereas joy arises from within." Inner joy is comforting and healthy for your soul. Do more of the things that bring you joy, and the life of your dreams is already yours.

Epiphany #12

CELEBRATE

Celebrate your victories in life for they create new ones, and remember to count your blessings daily. Write them down or say them aloud if you have to. It is highly recommended to continually reward yourself, and have fun throughout this process! There are small ways, and big ways we can reward ourselves. Recognizing the little things that create happiness for us are tangible ways that we can re-visit to bring more good things to us on a consistent basis. Buying that brand new car, you've always dreamed of, is a big way to celebrate. Sitting on a dock, overlooking the sunset, is a small way to celebrate. If we focus on the simple, free moments that make us feel good, we gain a better knowledge on what is truly important.

We've all heard the saying, "the best things in life are free." Well, the truth is...they are. When our happiness and freedom come with a price tag, we are putting value on our joy. Joy is abundant. It's all around us. Extract it from every moment because when you have the ability to do that, nothing can break you. You will become a master of manifestation. The world is yours! Life is an amazing journey, even in our darkest moments. Our realization that life is an ongoing celebration can be transforming. We understand that things will happen that are not to our liking, but how we perceive these situations is entirely up to us. When is the last time you rewarded yourself? When is the last time you did something which brought you a feeling of excitement? I'm talking about the feeling you had as a child when everything you did outside of your life felt like an adventure. When is the last time you went to see a blockbuster movie on opening day? When is the last time you left it all behind, and took a leap of faith to travel somewhere you've never been? When is the last time you told someone, this is not for me, and walked away?

Be wise, and have the freedom to be spontaneous. Have the knowledge that you can reach for the stars. Enjoy your journey because we only get one cycle of life at a time. Make yours a memorable one so you can carry that happiness over to the next life. Awakening to that simple reality is astonishing. Understanding that you can alter your reality is instrumental in manifestation. You were meant to travel and explore. You were meant to see the world in ways you can only imagine. And, imagination with action equals reality. The earth is our playground, and it can either be a paradise, or something else. Accepting that our reality is a paradise, for all our dreams to play out, is a pretty good indication of what you will create.

Those at the top are celebrating. They are celebrating because they have the knowledge that celebrating often, creates more things to celebrate about! Regardless of an individual's persona, they've uncovered a fundamental law of manifestation. That law is, whatever you envision life as being…is a mirror for the life you will live.

So start celebrating because you found this book, you're absorbing these tools, and you are eagerly ready to create something that coincides with your dreams. These mechanics are tested and proved. They are crafted to open you up to all kinds of possibilities deliberately. There is no specific course you have to take. Learn these concepts, and your reality will change. This book may lead you to another book, or perhaps a teacher. Rest assured, these ideas will bring you home. These components will bring you to the place you've always dreamed of, whatever that may be!

Maya Angelou wonderfully stated, "Life is not measured by the number of breaths we take, but by the moments that take our breath away." She knew that life was a celebration, and the more we see it as such, the more life will happen that way.

Epiphany #13

CLARITY

Christine Kane announced, "There's nothing quite as intense as the moment of clarity when you suddenly see what's really possible for you."

By definition, clarity means being coherent or having the ability to see easily. Why is clarity important to manifest your reality?

Life is unpredictable. Life can be challenging at times. With clarity, we handle life's challenges in a calm, simple manner. Clarity allows us to see through life's disappointments and roadblocks with ease. I'm talking about when you receive information that may not make you feel like the happiest person on earth. By being clear in your thoughts and trusting that all works to your benefit, those misfortunes are only seen as stepping stones. You come to a realization that nothing can truly harm you unless you allow it. No situation can bring you down unless you permit your thoughts to bring you to that place.

Clarity has enabled this book to be written. Clarity provides us tools to rise above any situation. Clarity shows the individuals you communicate with that you are listening and understand them. Clarity allows you to see the big picture in life. When it comes to manifesting, you first have to have an intention. But, intention intermingled with clarity is metamorphic. If you are clear about your visions, desires, and expectations, they will manifest faster, and will have longer lasting effects. I think about how life can be so awesome with clear intentions. Relationships, careers, and social interactions become healthier. Confusion and disagreement fade away with clarity. Clarity brings to light the benefits of every situation we encounter.

When we are clear, we are beacons of light. If we are communicating with someone, and we are being clear, conversations run smoother. If we are wanting to achieve something, clarity helps us achieve it. If we want to manifest something into our existence, clarity helps bring it to us sooner. Clarity reveals the "aha" moments where we see, understand, and get it!

Clarity of purpose is something that warrants discussion as well. We are all here for a reason. Personally, I am here to travel, enjoy life, and share the knowledge I have gained with others. My purpose is to bring positive energy to people, situations, and other environments. I carry that energy with me wherever I go. If you can identify your purpose and be clear about what it is you are here to do, then you have the ability to manifest whatever it is you want. You will be a manifestation machine. Thoughts will come into your mind, and will rapidly become your reality. Ideas about what you want to do, who you want in your life, and anything else that you wish will materialize quickly. The clearer you are, the more astonishing the results will be.

How do we get clear? Meditation, yoga, exercising, playing music, or creating art are just some ways that will help induce clarity. These methods are magnified with discipline and practice. The more time you place into these methods, the more clarity you will receive. We have many fancy medicines and drugs designed to help with clarity. But, I've witnessed the natural methods like meditation, yoga, exercising, music, and art work better than any pharmaceutical ever will.

The truth is, much of the confusion in our lives, and in our world, is due to lack of clarity. When we become clear, our nations are friendlier, our businesses run smoother, our relationships are better, and a beautiful reality can be created. So where does clarity come from? According to Sue Krebs, "Clarity comes from knowing what you want and moving in the direction of it. Your soul is guiding and supporting you every step of the way."

Indeed, we are guided. That guidance system operates at maximum capacity when we are clear. Setting guidelines for yourself in any situation will always help with clarity. Something I like to do, is pre-write emails. I do this all the time. If I'm responding to someone, I write the email and then save it to my drafts folder. I revisit this email a few times before I send it off. The reason I do this, is it allows me to be patient in my communication with others. More importantly, it gives me time to assess a situation before I just let a response fly into the ether. We use this same technique when actually speaking to one another. Before you say something, give yourself some time, or allow the other person some time to clarify, before you react with words. And how do we do that? We ask each other questions to gauge our next response.

Another cool way I use this technique is through manifestation. I will pre-write an email about a place that I'm at, how beautiful it is, what the weather was like BEFORE I actually experience it. I get as clear as I can in the email about what I'm doing. Then, I will save that email to my draft folder. I'll have you know that 100% of the time I will come to experience what I wrote about in that email. It becomes my reality! It's true. I do it all the time.

For example, right at this moment I have an email saved in my drafts to all my friends and family about the release of my book! It gives the title, where the book can be purchased, and a clear description. Guess what? I'm still in the process of actually writing my book. But, you can be sure in a few weeks I will be hitting the send button on that email that is saved in my draft folder! That's how this stuff works.

Our minds can be more at ease when we practice being clear. Our burdens will be lifted. Our conscience will be free. Moments of clarity will multiply as we build upon our practice. Think about how awesome life will be if you are clear in your choices and decision making. Life will be a walk in the park, and your reality will look much different than it does now. Your future will develop brightly based upon the clarity of your present choices. This is very powerful because it tells us that present confusion and chaos can be turned into something that helps us later on down the road. By having clarity of purpose, you are designing your reality at this very moment.

If you are reading these words and absorbing the message, your reality is in for a clear change.

Epiphany #14

CHANGE

Socrates said, "The secret of change is to focus all of your energy, not on fighting the old, but on building the new."

When I was a child, I remember my mother listening to an audio, self-improvement program day in and day out. That audio program was subliminally sending messages to our sub-conscious that change was ok. I am thankful for that, although at the time I felt it was weird. That program has allowed me to unknowingly cope well with change as I've progressed in life.

As I've grown and experienced what change does to people who have challenges with it, I am in awe at their resistance. People are scared of change. They resist anything that will get them out of their comfort zone or doing things in a different way. They are protective of their surroundings. This is why so many of us stay stagnant in mundane lifestyles. We have built-in mechanisms that put up walls when ideas or situations change our way of doing things. How can we live with the same habits, and expect different results? I'm here to tell you that life is better with change. Life is better when those walls come tumbling down. When we welcome change, it has the power to transform us and our circumstances.

Change is a driving force in Dream Mechanics. Change is completely necessary for you to create a new reality. Accept change as you move through your journey. Don't wait until you are so depleted by the norms, that you are uncomfortably forced into change. Embrace change with open arms! Change is a good, healthy thing. If you are reading this book, you want change. There may be something in your life that is not functioning properly, or perhaps you seek a fresh perspective. Maybe your current circumstances have you thinking about change. Change is strong when it happens internally because your exterior reality will change as a result. Embrace your fears, raise your consciousness, and change your life. Fear holds you back. Change propels you forward.

We are at a delicate time in our evolution, and in our current world affairs. Change is what is going to bring this world and people together. We are so desperate for it that we have to let go of all the things that we want to control, for it to fully bring us to the next level. With change comes new circumstances. A new reality can set in with the acceptance of change. Greater opportunities emerge with change. How can you manifest a new reality, if you are unwilling to change? Change is one of my favorite epiphanies. I love change, and I use it in my daily life to make things new and fresh. I use change in my career to forge new ideas, and handle different situations. I use change to see the bigger picture of my life. It is with change that we reach a higher state. And, in that higher state we can lift up ourselves, and be a springboard to help lift up others. With change, we can transition into a higher consciousness, and navigate any challenge.

I remember when change came to me in all its glory. Sometimes change turns a life upside down, but that is what some of us need to move us forward. Change brings a rebirth for those of us whose current circumstances no longer serve us. It was through the change process that I am able to write this book. Without change, the words you are reading on this piece of paper would not exist.

Change is a fundamental component in manifesting the reality you wish to create. It is inevitable that we must change our thoughts before our circumstances will change. We have to be willing to give up old ways of doing things. With a shift in our thought process, life can be altered into something greater. The metamorphosis can occur. Become an agent of change, in all that you do, because that is how we bring about a new status quo. That is how life will be more peaceful, and abundant for all of us. Without change, it's business as usual.

The late Wayne Dyer proclaimed, "Change your thoughts and change your life." When we put our thoughts on the new reality we wish to create, all the other "stuff" simply falls away. It's the attention we place, on the stuff we wish to avoid, that keeps it alive in us. We must move our thoughts on thinking why something is good for us in order to propel us forward. Thought manifestation, in Dream Mechanics, is established through change. Change how you are thinking, and you have the capacity to create a new life!

Epiphany #15

PEACE

Mahatma Gandhi said, "There is no way to peace. Peace is the way."

It took me awhile to wrap my head around that one. But, I started to think about it, and how it relates to Dream Mechanics. Can peace assist us in creating our reality? I believe it can.

Books, meditation practice, and gurus all teach us ways to be at peace. We are equipped to learn ways of being peaceful, but it is truly up to us to actually attain peace. Peace comes from simply being, and doing things in a mindful manner. Peacefulness in our speech and actions, at a slow and steady pace, is great wisdom. Moving through life with awareness creates peace in all that we do. Ultimately, peace is the embodiment of the word itself. It will do well to live in a way that is peaceful, rather than go through life in haste. In a peaceful way of existence, you can create a healthy life that goes along with that same ideology. Whatever you choose to create will exude that same sense of peacefulness.

Peace can come to us in a variety of ways, but intentionally creating a life of peace is divine. When is the last time you watched a sunrise or a sunset? When is the last time you moved through life in an unhurried manner? Writing this book has been a peaceful process, and it is my wish that peace emanate from the words as you read them. It was written in peaceful places overlooking majestic images of the Atlantic Ocean or contemplating in a sacred temple.

As a small child, raised in the concrete jungle of New York, I was conditioned to rush through everything. Today, I take the time to smell the flowers. I inhale their aroma to remind me that life is meant to be lived in the moment. I've also adopted a non-violent way of being, and simplified my life. Living in peace allows me to look at every situation through a different kind of lens. I can access challenging moments with fairness and neutrality. It will do us well to walk away from anything that diverts us from being at peace.

Over the last 10 years, I started to ask myself, why are we here? What is the purpose of this place we call Earth? It was at that moment that I was lead to a variety of teachers and belief systems. I've come to the conclusion that Earth is one big dream machine. It is a living, working organism just as we are. It is a habitat for dreamers, and a paradise for creators.

Upon a visit to the Sierra Nevada Mountains of Colombia, the peaceful Mamos taught us to care for this planet as if it were another human. The Kogi people explained to us who we really are, and the importance of living in a sustainable fashion. By being mindful and delicate with the Earth, I am living in the way of peace.

Contrary to popular belief, life is not a conflict. It's not a war. It is challenging to understand this concept because when we turn on the television all that is being reported about is turmoil and negativity. The reason this is happening is because most people are drawn to that. It's a respite from their own personal difficulties because they have yet to do the personal work to improve themselves. They are pulled into drama because it makes them feel normal. It's all they've come to know. And, that is what they put into their sub-conscious. And, that is what creates their reality. It is what they attract into their life experience. They bring those same emotions to their relationships, careers, schools, and social interactions.

Imagine if what we observed everyday was peaceful. Imagine when we turned on the television, the reporters were talking about situations of hope and love. Imagine if television shows were geared toward delivering positive messages. Then, that is what people will tune into, and that will be the frequency they will start to emit. Do yourself a favor, try to put good images, words, programs into your sub-conscious as much as you can. It will help you heal, and bring about peaceful feelings in your life.

Pema Chodron said, "Inner peace begins the moment you choose not to allow another person or event to control your emotions." Even in the face of the most challenging circumstances, we can remain poised and at peace. This is more powerful than money or fame, or anything else we can become intoxicated with. Peace and stillness amidst noise and chaos is elevating. Being able to remain at peace is the sign of a true life-master. Learn the art of peace, and the ability to stay calm, so you can create the reality you truly desire. Peace of mind begins with you. Choose peace!

Epiphany #16

MOTIVATION

Charles Ajero said, "Motivation helps you prepare your mind, helping you get ready, get set, and go for your dreams."

Most people have challenges living their dreams because they require proper motivation. They become comfortable with their present circumstances, and settle for it. They have all the ideas of what they desire, but to achieve them is just wishful thinking. Some of us often fall short of our opportunities due to lack of motivation.

So, what exactly is motivation? According to a Google search, "Motivation is literally the desire to do things." I would just add, the desire to do things WITH EXCITMENT. Why do we need motivation to create our reality? Well, if you're sitting at home wondering why your dreams are not manifesting, it's time to get up and take action! Taking action allows you to move in the direction of your dreams. We can self-motivate to take action in a variety of ways. I self-motivate by being sure I make room for balance in my life. The way I do this is by allotting time to remove myself from my present circumstances. I do this in small, effective ways. I will go to a movie, randomly walk around the city, or dine at a local restaurant that I've never been too. I also make time to meditate so I can expand my consciousness. This small practice has manifested into visiting all 7 continents, all 50 states, and all 7 wonders of the world!

Simply stated, it is wise to get out of your comfort zone and try new things. I've never realized how challenging this can be for individuals because I started doing it at a very young age. At the tender age of 19, I left the nest and moved out west to go to college and eventually start a career. Most people will patronize the same places over and over again because it feels safe. They'll live in the same neighborhoods because it feels familiar. It's all they know. There is a really simple way to motivate yourself, and it can be done when you begin to explore. You can do this on a very small scale right now. If you're planning on going to dinner this weekend, go to a place you've never been before. Just the act of going out for dinner can be motivating for some.

When you wake up in the morning, sit up, smile and say, "I am excited for this new day!" Get on the side of optimism, and your life will change drastically. Smile for no apparent reason at all, and laugh even when there is nothing to laugh about. Love as much as you can. Eat chocolate, in moderation, on a daily basis because it gets the endorphins moving you to a happy state. Listen to some inspiring music, or go see a masterpiece of art at a local gallery. There are numerous ways to get pumped up about life!

And, when fear or doubt start to poke their way into your mind, to keep you where you are…embrace them, and then talk yourself through them in a positive manner. Replace the thoughts of fear and doubt with courage and inspiration. As soon as the thoughts that keep you stuck start trickling in, feed your mind with anything that represents happiness, laughter, and love. Read a book that transmits a positive message, or look up an inspiring quote about life. Switch your mindset because if you don't those thoughts will build upon one another, and you will become stuck in your habituated ways of being. The only way to form new habits and break free from negativity, is to motivate yourself! Be proactive in your approach with everyone and everything.

Jim Rohn said, "Motivation is what gets you started. Habit is what keeps you going." If we can break free from old habits to open ourselves up to better ones, our motivation will continually grow.

Happiness breeds joyfulness. Hope breeds peace. Get in the habit of filling your mind with positive thoughts. We are beings of light who are here to celebrate life in all its' glory. Know this, trust this, and believe this. Through motivation, we can create a reality that coincides with what we envision for ourselves. There is a certain amount of action that will be required of each individual to live their dream, and motivation puts you in that proper state of action. Action infused with motivation is a powerful force in Dream Mechanics.

Epiphany #17

POSITIVITY

"Beautiful things happen when you distance yourself from negativity." - Unknown.

Positivity is your direct pathway to manifesting your reality. If anything else, go into every situation with a positive outlook. Turn every challenging situation you face into one where you, or the other individuals involved, can learn something from one another. What does it mean to be positive? Being positive means we are free from worry and doubt. We become a conduit for happy energy where good vibrations can flow. We expect favorable results in all that we do. We are clear, and have an encouraging effect on our lives, and the lives of others. We deliberately use positive framing in speech and tone. Positive framing is asking the same exact thing in a non-demanding or threatening way. For example, if someone is doing something that doesn't align with you, instead of saying "stop that," you say, "would it be ok if you assist me by not doing that?" Basically, you recruit the other person in finding a peaceful resolution rather than issue an ultimatum. You will be surprised by the results you will achieve. I use this in my personal life, and in my business dealings. It takes a few more seconds in your thought process, but it will prove to be beneficial for you in the long run. Be conscious of the words you choose to use.

Greet everyone with a smile, and do your best to leave them with one regardless of the circumstances. Think of every smile you give as karmic currency that increases your bank account to pay for the reality you wish to create. The key word in that previous sentence is...give. Giving of yourself whether it be in the form of a smile, time, money, or energy puts you in the position to have the dream work its' magic for you.

Being positive emanates from you, and your vibrational output will exude a certain feeling that people will knowingly or unknowingly pick up on. Positivity shines through in your face and body language. It even has the ability to come through in your texts, emails, and books! All of the epiphanies mentioned in this book are presented in a positive manner both consciously and intentionally.

According to Wikipedia, "Positive psychology is the branch of psychology that uses scientific understanding and effective intervention to aid in the achievement of a satisfactory life." Consider this book to be an intervening entity to awaken you to a path of recovery. There is a positive thought movement happening at this very moment. We are waking up to the idea that life flourishes when we think outside of the box. I'm talking about seeing the glass half full, and lifting each other up. A positive attitude is contagious. It is the source of greatness. When you master positivity, you have taken back an innocent part of your life where you grant yourself permission to be happy. In being positive, you reconnect to a child-like mindset and way of being. Remember the days where you didn't have a care in the world. The world didn't seem to throw so much at you, and your ego wasn't as developed. That mental state of bliss is where you want to be. It is from there that you can move mountains. You can create anything! Your imagination starts to run wild again, and anything is possible!

Being positive is liberating. Positivity frees you from any situation that does not feel good. Your positive feelings will start to shift when things take a turn and do not feel right. That is your trigger to get back on track. Either make the situation work better for you, or remove yourself from it completely. Your inner guidance system is built to move you in the direction of your dreams if you can effectively discern how it works. If you follow the instructions in this book, you will be on the path of your dreams in no time. These are simple, useful tips on taking your life back from a phase of blindness and drama. It's as if you had the download with you all along, but didn't have the proper program to open it up. Now you do! Positivity begins with you. Change begins with you. If you work on yourself, you will create a better life. You will then be a beacon for others to create a better life, and the cycle will begin to shift for all of us.

Some small activities that will shift you into a better state of being are meditation, reading material that inspires you, or taking a walk in nature. Optimism is about being cheerful, and envisioning a spectacular existence. It is about choosing your attitude given any set of circumstances which elevates you to another level. Positivity is another key component of Dream Mechanics. When you realize that everything that happens to you is a result of the choices you make, then we start making choices that serve our greater good. Have a sunny disposition, put a positive spin on what you say, and the rest will take care of itself. Positivity allows you to see the good in all, and the bright side of everything!

Deepak Chopra said, "You can't make positive choices for the rest of your life without an environment that makes those choices easy, natural, and enjoyable." Take inventory of your environment. Is what you have surrounded yourself with a good place to make choices? Do you feel supported by those around you? This pertains to the individuals you interact with, the careers you part-take in, and the home life you have created. Environment is directly connected to the creation of our reality. In order for us to create successfully, we want to be in an atmosphere that approves of our choices on a very deep level.

Epiphany #18

PERSEVERANCE

"Great works are performed, not by strength, but by perseverance" – Samuel Johnson.

As a teenager, I remember walking on the streets of the humble neighborhood I grew up in. One day as I meandered along, sitting atop a pile of trash, as if it was specifically placed there for me to see, was a brand new framed picture of the word...Perseverance. I immediately grabbed that picture for some reason. That picture would eventually go with me to college, and hang on my wall. It was a constant reminder of what it means to persevere. Although, I really didn't know what the word meant, I was drawn to the image in the picture. It was an image of a rock climber hanging from the side of a splendid mountain about half way to the top. By looking at the picture every day, the word perseverance was embedding itself into my sub-conscious on a consistent basis.

So what does perseverance mean? "Perseverance is the continued effort to do something despite difficulty, failure, or opposition" (Merriam-Webster). It is achieving success regardless of the obstacles we face, and the key to unlocking our true potential. As I look back on my life, it behooves me just how awesome my life experience has been. There have been countless times when I was discouraged by a friend, a family member, or certain life circumstances. But, as the definition says, it's a matter of breaking through the barriers or difficulties that life presents to us which enables individuals to persevere. Perseverance is the courage to prevail and triumph during times of crisis. Challenges will come in the form of situations, people, and other life drama. When we persevere, we get knocked down, but we get back up. We develop the skills to enhance our life experience regardless of difficulties. We re-invent ourselves as we aspire to reach new destinations. We become enlightened, and we discover our life's purpose. We relentlessly focus on the positive, and we move forward in our journey. We beat the odds even when they are stacked against us. We ultimately fulfill our destiny.

It is this right way of thinking that secures us the know-how to create our reality. We have the ability to persevere through things like bullying, abuse, neglect, fear, and conflict. We can shift to a place of happiness, transcendence, and peace. With the spirit of perseverance comes the endurance of faith. And, with that faith comes our safe haven to live our dreams. We have to eliminate the notion to dramatize situations, and live in a way that keeps us resilient. Perseverance keeps us doing a task until we can achieve our goal. If your goal is to change your reality, than perseverance is going to get you there. It is with tenacity and sheer will power that we can keep getting battered until we eventually persevere.

David Sarnoff claimed, "The will to persevere is often the difference between failure and success." Failure is not a stopping point, it is a tipping point to live out your dreams. We are limitless beings who have unlimited potential to carry out our wishes. The more we recognize this innate quality in all of us, the better off we all will be.

I am so happy I came across that picture that someone was throwing away all those years ago. The value it bestowed upon me was priceless. And, the funny thing is I didn't even have to pay for it. That picture was given to me freely. In fact, many things have been mysteriously given to me on my journey. Those things or people or places that come to us, seemingly from nowhere, are really there for a reason. Recognize them, honor them, and understand their purpose. For when you do, you will have received a special gift that is given to those who want to consciously change their reality, and improve their circumstances. Any of us can realize this ability, no matter who we are, or what background we come from.

The truth is. . .we can have it all. Through unwavering perseverance, we can attain the most magnificent reality.

Medi
tat
ion

Epiphany #19

MEDITATION

Sri Chinmoy proclaimed, "Meditation means the recognition or discovery of one's own true self."

Meditation changes lives. Meditation allows us to get to a very special place within ourselves, and the environment we are surrounded with. While a yoga practice is just as helpful, I can honestly speak on meditation because I practice it daily. What started out with me unable to sit still for more than five minutes has turned into a 40-minute daily ritual. I center myself, either through a guided meditation that I listen to, or with a teacher in an actual meditation class. By the way, if you are blessed to become a student of a teacher, then this method is often preferred.

Meditation balances our energy and soothes our spirit. Meditation enhances our mind, and regenerates our body naturally. Our long-term memory becomes better. The way we handle everyday challenges becomes stronger. Meditation is a huge component in Dream Mechanics. It is required for the true student to have some form of therapy that allows their mind to rest. Now, I'm not talking about when you sleep because even while we sleep our minds our working. I'm speaking about a dedicated time where you are focusing only on your breath, and the connection to everything around you. This daily practice adjoined with loving kindness, insight (vipassana), or equanimity meditation changes how you perceive the world around you. You will find yourself having unparalleled levels of energy and calmness. You will make better decisions in life, and have clarity of mind. You will start to take joy in waiting, and become a student of patience. When we meditate, we connect with the universal field. Our thoughts begin to slow and our mind becomes more concentrated.

The mind is comparable to a muscle, and it requires exercise. I believe you have to work at meditation for it to have long lasting, positive effects. Maxwell Maltz said, "It takes 21 days to form a new habit." Making meditation a habit is more likely to be one of the best decisions of your life. Now, meditation may or may not resonate with you, and yoga is another alternative. I have friends who look and feel amazing with a daily yoga practice, and both forms of practice go hand-in-hand. If you develop a meditation or yoga practice, you will be amazed at the results!

Experimenting with hallucinogens or other stuff can be risky. I promise you that with practice, meditation and yoga can bring you to the same place you seek to reach naturally. They have been a major tradition of the East for thousands of years. There is a reason for that. There is power in silence and stillness. In our material-driven, be busy society, meditation is transforming. Meditation is the thread that connects all of the epiphanies that are described in this book. It is the one common denominator for all of them.

I was raised in a very different environment than how I live today. Meditation has healed me in more ways than one. It helps with our visualizations, and aids in creating our reality. The manifestation process is accelerated with a good meditation practice because it disseminates all the clutter. Most of us have challenges with manifestation because we haven't identified ways to get clear. Meditation is the remedy for that because it enhances your consciousness.

So how does one begin a meditation practice? There are teachers from all over the globe that want to share their method with students. Do some research in your area, and I'm sure something will pop up. Find local retreats that you can attend. Many retreats offer some type of silence or meditation instruction to help you unplug. A good retreat will insist that technology not be used because it is a time for contemplation. These retreats will have immense benefits to your mind and operating system. You will be able to download and absorb more with a good meditation practice. Most of us formulate a meditation practice so we can reconnect with the very basic part of ourselves. We induce a state of bliss and centeredness through meditation. Happiness is what we are all searching for, and meditation is a clever method of tapping into eternal bliss. Essentially, meditation enables us to nurture our spiritual growth.

Recently, I watched a you-tube video about an elementary school. The school has begun sending children to meditation class rather than detention if they do something wrong. WOW! This is such a progressive, alternative way to re-focus negative behavior into something positive. The benefits that these children will reap will be wonderful. Meditation will transform their bitterness into peacefulness and calm. Meditation is the liberation for the habits of our minds. Buddha was asked, "What have you gained from meditation?" He replied, "Nothing! However, let me tell you what I lost: Anger, Anxiety, Depression, Insecurity, Fear of old age, and Death."

Epiphany #20

DIET

"Your body is a reflection of who you are. If you want to look healthy, you will have to be healthy (hasfit.com)." The right diet will aid in digesting the components of Dream Mechanics. Having the appropriate mental diet is just as important as a physical one. Mentally, we want to fill our minds with thoughts of love, harmony, and ease.

As a vegetarian, it is imperative to cleanse the system, and then be mindful of what we put into the body temple. Veganism or vegetarianism is a healthier way to live. Your face becomes softer, and your complexion becomes lighter with this type of diet. Protein sources are often required, but your body will love you. Your appearance will change completely. You will look younger and more vibrant because the exterior reflects the interior.

Deep in Northern India, it was explained to me like this. If we are eating animals and fish, they both have a consciousness. Therefore, you are consuming the consciousness and feelings of what that animal and fish were experiencing when their lives ended. This explains our societal challenges, and labels such as attention deficit order, emotional disturbance, hyper disorder, and the list goes on and on. Studies have shown that diet has a direct correlation with how we are feeling. If we are loading our system with meat and carnivorous material, we are loading it with all of their emotions plus our own! We are what we eat, and what you eat directly effects your emotions. Think about the age of the dinosaurs. There were carnivore and herbivore dinosaurs. Think of all the children's books you read as a child. The carnivores were blood thirsty, hunters. The plant eating herbivores seemed to always be at peace. It's a funny analogy, but it's true!

Our bodies fascinate me. They are so intricate, and whoever designed them was on another level all together. Think about what is happening in your body right now. Think about everything that is running through it, and all that makes up the body. Be mindful of what you literally put in your body today. Do you feel happy, do you have unlimited energy, and are you at ease? If none of these apply, then seriously consider what your intake is. Like a car, our body vehicle will run at maximum performance depending on the quality of ingredients that go into it. Synthetic oils make a car run smoother, and impact the car's life capacity. It's the same concept when it comes to diet and human bodies. We will run smoother as a result of what we are ingesting.

The organic movement in the food industry is happening for a reason. My suggestion is to eat and live organically. The health-conscious alternatives that are being promoted are to create awareness around the heavy use of chemical ingredients. Today, people have information at their fingertips. Be mindful of the ingredients in the items you bring into your home. Be conscious of what you are supplying your children with to nourish themselves. The diet is something that had to be included in this book because it matters. As a teacher, I believe diet has an impact on learning and behavior, especially for children. Diet, accompanied with regular exercise, has our minds and operating systems running at optimal levels. We want to move through this world in our best form. With the proper form, we can attract and create a reality that is healthy in a variety of aspects. Our temperament will be gentle as a result of a good diet, and our energy will be greater.

Understanding personal energy is a pre-requisite for Dream Mechanics. We are all energy, and our energy is greatly determined by our diet. The science of Ayurveda has been curing and caring for people for thousands of years. The system is based upon the five elements of ether, air, fire, water, and earth. There is much we can do by incorporating Ayurveda in our diet and reality. Also, acupuncture is another eastern philosophical approach to healing and well-being. Acupuncture helps balance our system so that it will flow harmoniously. Both of these methods combined with a good diet are catalysts for creating a healthy reality.

Epiphany # 21

CHARITY

Matthieu Richard said, "The greater the social awareness and charitable involvement, the greater is the happiness of the citizen." Charity is kindness and compassion in action. Giving back aids in the manifestation process, especially when you do not expect anything in return. Being benevolent and displaying a kind heart is good for all of us. When you give from your heart, especially when it is not premeditated, it returns to you in ways that are uncalculated and unfathomable. The joy of giving opens doors to a universal bank account. You never know when it will come back to you, or in what capacity, but it does return. You will also be helping humanity, and realize that your personal challenges are minor compared to the challenges of others. Perform some volunteer work in an area you always wanted to learn about. It could very well turn into a career path that you love. Serve at soup kitchens during the holidays or any day for that matter. Putting yourself in service to others allows you to recognize and be grateful for all you have. Give a talk at your local rotary or lions club. You'll be surprised how much your life experience can help others. You'll also be amazed at how well you can teach.

Charitable works are done by all of our greatest visionaries and agents of change around the world. Both in past and future, those who give of themselves eventually come to the realization that they are greater than themselves. Join a fellowship where you work toward a common purpose in lifting the social challenges we face as a society or globally. In doing so, you will remove yourself from your everyday routine to help another human being for no reason whatsoever. You will consciously join the collective whole in our pursuit for peace. This type of thinking and action is beautiful. It builds confidence in manifesting the reality you wish to create. By giving of your time, energy, money, or services, you enlighten others.

In my travels, I began making it a habit to visit orphanages or bring gifts to the places I was blessed to visit. There are also simple easy ways of doing charitable acts. Daily random acts of kindness are a good place to start as well! Begin by opening the door for someone behind you when entering a shop. Leave an extra twenty percent on your next restaurant bill. Donate blood at a local blood drive. Donate food at a local food pantry. Provide clothing to a neighborhood collection bin. These simple acts are transforming. They put you in the mindset of helping your fellow human. Manifestation thrives on this type of mentality.

Try a "give to live" program. For the next thirty days, do something or give something of yourself each day. You will find that you're better at doing this than you think. You will begin to find ways, to be a source of good, as the thirty days progresses. New ideas will randomly come to you on how you can make a contribution. You will tap into the universal consciousness, and be a servant of its magic. Oh and by the way, it feels incredibly wonderful to give!

Gary Inrig mentioned, "Generosity is a practical expression of love." Power in the form of money and status is never permanent. But, being a giving soul goes beyond lifetimes. It taps into the unseen force that moves through all of us. Generosity is rooted in a special understanding of the thread that connects us all. Many of our most successful individuals become our greatest philanthropists. Imagine if we can all be philanthropists on a very basic level. The world would be such a better place. Give what you can to help others. The opportunities to do so are endless, and are much needed in our world. Giving back opens up a vacuum to create a reality that is filled with love, kindness, and abundance.

Epiphany #22

DETACHMENT

There are many ways in which we become entangled with life, and each other. We form attachments from the moment we are detached at birth. Attachments come in the form of emotional, physical, and mental capacities. Emotional attachments can have an effect on your well-being, especially if you are dependent on happiness from outside circumstances. The moment you realize that your emotions are yours, is the moment your break free from emotional dependency.

We start to form emotional attachments during our early developmental stages. As a child, we become upset when something is taken from us. Or, cry if we are told to do something that doesn't agree with us. We take pleasure when things go our way, and feel frustrated when they don't. We act out of emotion because it is what we observe in our home environment, on television, internet, and social media apps. We often act out because we are never taught how to balance our emotions in an authentic manner. To do so is to recognize, that like everything, emotions are not permanent. They are forever changing. When we grasp this concept, we can easily move from one emotion to the next emotion with ease. We can even concentrate on specific emotions that we enjoy in order to attract more of those emotions to us.

In a physical sense, we become attached to our friends, family, and belongings. Everything has an invisible thread. The world–wide web is one big attachment. It is connecting everything and everyone in ways that shape our existence. But, there is a fundamental difference in being connected and connecting with someone. You can connect with someone on a level that is mutually beneficial for you both. When you are connected, you are plugged into a stream of consciousness that can create challenges and impulses. We are all connected, but this doesn't mean that those connections should determine our state of being. If they do, then you are connecting in a way that may not be healthy. On a mental level, we become attached to our career and certain relationships. These attachments eventually breed hardship because they become chains of dependency rather than links of joy.

What does all this have to do with manifestation and creating your reality? Detach from the things and individuals that bind you. Anything or anyone that prevents you from spreading your wings deserves careful analysis. This is a life lesson that many do not grasp, even as we are completing a life cycle. I'd like you to consider the next questions carefully. Do we take anything with us when we die? Do we take our relationships, material possessions, children, or careers with us? These areas are a means to our happiness in this life-time, and if they are not, then it is important to accept them as an element of the journey and nothing more. It is far easier to move through life with detachment in mind then it is to move through it otherwise.

Detachment helps us flourish. It allows us to be mindful of what and who we entangle ourselves with. You are here to live a life of joy and abundance. That is your birthright! Worrying, anxiety, and fear come from being attached. We get attached to people and places. But, the moment we realize we are free to roam the world is when we unlock the chains that bind us. That is the moment we are truly free. Creating your reality comes from knowing that we have the freedom to do so. We are not products of our circumstances or environments. We are beings of light that have unlimited potential to do, and design as we wish. When we are constantly worrying about something or someone that does not make us feel good, that is a sign to detach. When something has consumed all of our time and energy that is a trigger to detach. Dwelling on things that are outside of your control, is a signal to detach. When a job or a career has become the only thing we can think about, that is our time to detach. We are endless, just like the horizon. If anything compromises the integrity of that expansiveness, or attempts to bind us in anyway, detachment is our resolution. You will go on living the same reality if you're attached to everything in it. We must detach from the thought patterns that we cling to in order to produce new results.

Enlightenment is derived from being detached. This is a fundamental aspect of Dream Mechanics. Reality will begin to change as you realize the things that you need to detach from. When in doubt, detach. It's as simple as that. Detachment is a self-assessment tool that enables us to manifest our dreams in an effective manner.

Epiphany #23

TRUST

Trust is a firm belief in the integrity, ability, or character of a person or thing. What does it mean to trust in the process? I remember someone saying this to me and hearing these words in a variety of self-improvement arenas. It is very simple. When doubt comes streaming into your mind, or all the thoughts on why you can't do something occur…STOP. Literally, stop the thoughts in their tracks, and trust that you are being guided to something you are supposed to do. Focus on all the reasons why you WANT to do something. Write them down on a piece of paper, or record them in your cell phone. We have already identified that we have an inner guidance system which we can trust. Follow the nudges that are being presented to you. It is your duty to do so. Those nudges aren't coming from no-where. They are coming from a very special place. It is our responsibility to recognize them, and act on them. If we don't move in the direction of our nudges, we are giving our dreams away to other circumstances.

This is really powerful stuff to absorb. Most of us aren't doing what we are required to do in order to manifest the reality we desire. It's as if our creative process was slowly taken away from us in school systems, work environments, or even personal relationships. I'm telling you to trust in the ideas that come to you. Trust in the places you envision going. Trust that the money will come. Trust that the means, to achieve whatever is being downloaded into your mind, is achievable because all of those thoughts happen for a reason. Part of manifesting is to trust the things you visualize will manifest. Trust is the most challenging aspect for people to grasp. Trust is a hurdle to overcome in the human condition all together. But, having the capacity to trust is transformational because it determines our creations. Your life experience, the traumas you've endured, and the situations that have been presented to you will often be a result of your trust factor. If you could put all that "stuff" aside, and raise your trust factor, then the sky is the limit.

Trust is a powerful epiphany that enables us to create our reality. I know it can be challenging to trust a situation, or a person, or an event that on the surface appears to be harmful. But, have no fear. Even those situations, when trusted, provide valuable clues in creating our reality. Ernest Hemingway proclaimed, "The best way to find out if you can trust somebody is to trust them." Trust everyone. And if you ever find yourself in a place where you don't know who or what to trust, then simply trust yourself.

Self-trust is the single most important aspect in creating a new reality. So many of us get upset when we don't get what we want. Sometimes those situations are for our greater good. See the big picture! Know that you are safe in every moment. Don't allow fear or doubt to blur your ability to trust. We are wise beings, and our higher self always wants what is best for us at all times. Trust in that! Have faith in the unseen by knowing that everything works out for us no matter what. We are conditioned to have a plan from the time we go to school. School teachers are also conditioned to have a plan. Plan for this, and plan for that. It is all conditioning at its best. And when things don't go as planned, well we all can relate to what happens next. Throw most of the plan out the window, and leave room for the divine to work its magic. Learn what it feels like when plans fall through so you can easily bounce back and co-create. Leave room for the bliss that comes from being unstructured. Allow life to unfold organically, and you will be amazed at the results!

Epiphany #24

SIMPLICITY

Leonardo Da Vinci said, "Simplicity is the ultimate form of sophistication."

Many prominent individuals we meet, or read about, have mastered the art of simplicity. They are no smarter than you and me, but they've eliminated complexity in all forms, and their life is a reflection of happiness as a result.

Simplicity is my favorite epiphany. Calm and simple has become my life's mantra. What does it mean to be simple? First, being simple is an acquired skill. It will take some effort to simplify our speech, relationships, and environment. But, once you do, the rewards are endless. Simplicity is cutting through all the confusion in your life. It's knowing that the answers we seek are all around us. It's looking at every situation with a solution-oriented outlook. And understanding a minimalist outlook determines our life experience.

To put it simply, we are guided. The universe coordinates the experiences of billions of people not to mention itself without missing a beat. Gaining the insight that our life is designed is instrumental in Dream Mechanics. Life puts you right where you need to be. There is a certain geometry to life just as in the cosmos.

Even if you take a detour, there is a reason for it. Everything we do, everything we say is part of a very simple design to deliver us to the reality we are creating. Have less, do more, and be more is a sure fire way to get us there. Why is behaving in a simple manner so challenging for many of us to comprehend?

One of my favorite avatars, Richard Bronson said this, "Complexity is your enemy. Any fool can make something complicated. It is hard to keep things simple." Being around monks for the last seven years has taught me quite a lot about being simple. I understand that simplicity is where we find the joy in life. Being simple keeps our mind clear, and our conscience free. Many teachers have graced me with their presence over the last few years. It has been a great blessing to have been exposed to some of the greatest teachers on our planet. They all agree that simplicity is the fabric of a happy life. And, for all those who have been taught to have a sense of urgency, I'm sorry to tell you, but that was conditioning in all its glory. The system we are a part of wants you in an anxious state. Worry and anxiety feed a very ill-mannered cycle that some have learned to prosper from. I'm here to tell you that life is not a rush. We are not supposed to be in a hurry or busy. In fact, life is a pleasant journey of one step at a time. Once we grasp, a slow and steady approach, then the cycle of life becomes much easier to navigate. We feel more alive and much less pressure. Days and nights begin to flow, and we are gifted a sense of peace throughout them. Sleeping becomes enjoyable because our conscience is carrying less of a burden.

Through simplicity we learn one of life's greatest lessons. The lesson we learn is to honor life in a way that moves us calmly and efficiently. We start to do all of our daily tasks in a conscious, mindful manner. Every activity we take part in is done with awareness and focus. Every conversation is important. Every movement is relative to our physical and mental well-being. As I type the words of this book, I am doing so with simplicity and ease. Whatever we are doing in life will reflect that same energy. We will bring that element to all that we do and create. Simplicity is vital to the health of our soul. It is essential in creating a new reality. Becoming simple will require breaking the deep-rooted habits you've formed throughout your life. It will mean that you will steer clear of drama and pettiness because they promote discord. Happiness, contentment, and peace of mind are found in the simple things. These are the feelings we strive for when living our dreams. These attributes are necessary to break free, and live a life of immense proportions.

Do yourself a favor, and start to simplify everything in your entire life right now.

Epiphany #25

FREE WILL

Free thinkers change the world. Aeschylus said, "And one who is just of his own free will shall not lack for happiness; and he will never come to utter ruin."

Free will is required for Dream Mechanics. If you are of your own free will, you are living a life that is not dictated by anyone or any situation. You have all the time in the world. The journey is yours regardless of what happens.

Free will enables you to live the life of your dreams. You are no longer a slave to the grind. You are a master manifester who recognizes that you are responsible for your happiness. Anything that is not serving the creation you wish to see for yourself must be cast aside. I know millionaires who are imprisoned by their circumstances. Whether you are rich or poor does not matter if you are not free. Freedom to be who you are, create the life you wish, and live that incredible version of yourself is epic. Freedom is the ability to act, speak, or think without hindrance or restraint. With freedom, you will be a person who is experiencing life rather than suffering in it. You will be an illuminated being of light, and your soul will belong to you again. You will never be a victim of life's circumstances, or succumb to those who wish to see you do anything but succeed. You realize that it all starts with you! The life you want, the environment you want, and the journey you wish to part-take in begins and ends with you.

Free will is the ability to choose between possible courses of action, and impart your god-giving right to do as you wish. It is complete freedom of action. This is an enlightening concept to grasp. You choose the course of action, not your paycheck, your partner, or your circumstances. ONLY YOU! And the beautiful thing about free will is there are many pathways that you can take to exhibit its' potential. You just have to select the pathway that moves you forward in the direction of your dreams, and not the one that keeps you where you are. Examine your current circumstances to see if what has been created is done of your own free will. If there are any portions of your life experience which do not articulate your freedom, then change them immediately. If you are in a situation which binds you, or feels restricted, that is a clue to impart your free will. Exercise free will, and it will carry over into all that you do. Your life will feel more natural as a result, and you will feel that you are creating life rather than being controlled by it. You will be the captain of your fate. By directing your free will, you can build a new environment.

Free will is not to be confused with destiny. We will cover destiny at the end of this book. There is a difference between free will and destiny. Sri Sri Ravi Shankar said, "Life is a combination of destiny and free will. Rain is destiny; whether you get wet or not is free will!" Free will gives us power to choose. The first act of creating your reality is to simply believe in free will. Believe in your ability to live the life of your dreams.

We are the product of the thoughts that go on in our mind. Choose the good thoughts to break free of hereditary patterns. Choose to live in a way that makes you feel good. Far too often our free will is compromised in our personal lives, and in the society in which we find ourselves. Our institutions, careers, and societal norms often suppress our birthright to be free. We have become conditioned to live out a life that is expected of us, rather than living a life of our expectations. Plato's Allegory of the Cave had a profound impact on my journey. It inspired me to live the way in which I choose. It was the driving force for including this particular epiphany. We must grant ourselves freedom, and then re-learn how to use it in life so we may share that knowledge with others.

"A free man is someone who follows his dreams, and turns them into reality" – Unknown.

Epiphany #26

BELIEF

Jacqueline Purcell said, "You must unlearn what you have been programmed to believe since birth. That software no longer serves you if you want to live in a world where all things are possible."

Some of us were fortunate to be raised with a set of proper beliefs from the time we were children. Some of us were given the task to formulate those beliefs, on our own, as we experienced life. Do our belief systems actually serve us? Family and religious beliefs can be of use to us as we progress in our spiritual endeavors. But, if you really want to uncover the life of your dreams, it will do you well to examine your current beliefs, and re-establish them. Your belief system dictates your reality. Much of our reality is based upon our beliefs. A belief system is the foundation or the blueprint of one's life. With a good foundation, the individual can withstand strong challenges along the way. Like a building, we are a structure of the same nature. Buildings can rise into the stratosphere. We can as well. Buildings can be built to stand the test of time. So can we. I use this metaphor to stress the importance of a good belief system.

Although I was raised Catholic, I didn't choose that belief system for myself. I remember attending classes and learning about various biblical accounts. But, there was no connection for me.

These early beliefs served a purpose, but they did not prepare my soul for the journey of life. That revelation came later in life when I embarked upon the spiritual path. Whenever that moment of conversion shall come for you, or under whatever circumstances it shall arise, it is imperative for your life experience. I am grateful that it came when it did for me because it gave me a sense of depth and substance. When I look back, I am fortunate for all I have endured. The challenging moments that we pass through in our lives bring us closer to where we want to be, and sets the tone for where we are going. I believe that I will carry the lessons that this universe has presented to me into my next life. Ultimately, I will be a better person because of them.

Believing is a major part of the creative process. All religions teach this, and that key aspect resonates with me. What I would like to present to you is to have the ability to truly believe again! Believe as if you were a child once more. Believe that your dreams can manifest, right here in this moment, on this plane of existence. You don't have to go to heaven to realize all you wish for. You can have your dreams right now. There is a certain amount of recapitulation that one must attune too. With this turning of the dial, we can re-formulate our belief system to serve us in a more joyful and practical manner. What I have found is that mind and belief must be in harmony. If you can get the two to work with one another, the results are astounding.

When I was a child, I often heard people say, "Seeing is believing." This implied: show me, and then I will believe you. As I've matured in life, I understand that, "believing is seeing." This simple reversal of words implies: believe, and it will manifest. Therefore, with a certain level of belief we have the capability to manifest all we want to see. Belief is the preamble to manifestation. You have to believe in your dreams so you can bring them into existence.

Use your imagination to conjure the feelings for manifestation. Sometimes it's wise to throw the book out the window, and believe with a certain level of purity. Accepting that we are primarily responsible for creating our life is a core belief. The universe has precise laws that can serve us when we are in-tune to its frequency. Most of what we manifest is a direct result of our thoughts and belief system. Learning how that system operates, and using it to our benefit, is a valuable tool in Dream Mechanics.

George Seaton said, "Faith is believing in things when common sense tells you not too."

Epiphany #27

TRUTH

John 8:32 says, "Then you will know the truth, and the truth will set you free (NIV)."

These words rang true for me in all their glory, and they will for you as well. The bible is one of the best known self-improvement books in existence. As a spiritual individual, I believe there is a universal truth to many of our religious books.

Being true to yourself and others is going to create a shift in your awareness, and help you develop your desired reality. Standing in truth means that you aren't afraid to assess your situation, and ask the difficult questions. Truth allows you to evaluate your situation, and really see if it is moving you in the direction of your dreams or not. It's as simple as that. Are you creating the life you wish to create? Are you doing what you really want to be doing? Answering these questions, truthfully and simply, will help guide you in the direction of your dreams. Truth requires self-discipline. Standing in truth means that things are pretty black and white. Steer clear of those gray areas because they often breed confusion and chaos. Remain in the light of truth, and our experience becomes more enjoyable. Be conscious of your speech, and how you respond to the inquiries of the world.

All too often we take our word for granted, but our word is our bond. Miguel Ruiz professed, "Be impeccable with your word." The reason for this belief is that our speech is powerful. It sends signals to other individuals and the universe about our intentions and how we feel.

If you are creating your reality, you will soon realize that much of it will be based on what you say to yourself, but also what you proclaim to others. Therefore, it is crucial that our word be truthful because that will affect the creation. Truth is self-discipline that allows us to live an open and harmonious life. We want to be beacons of light who add illumination to our world. Truth exposes you to vulnerability, but keeps you free from fear in the process. We want to feel free and fearless so our manifestations can come to fruition in a healthy manner.

The Buddha said, "Three things cannot be long hidden. The sun, the moon, and the truth." We must live and create from a place of truthfulness. Being truthful empowers us. We will shed any heavy burdens that we carry by being truthful. The lighter we are, the better we will be able to flow with the stream of life. The better we will be able to create a reality that encompasses abundance. Truthfulness is an anecdote to all that pervades us. We have to get truthful about how we feel about our present circumstances in order to change our reality. This is a vital aspect of Dream Mechanics. Truth levels the playing field of life, and allows us to forge a new path. Truth enables us to take an honest assessment of our life, and make the necessary adjustments to manifest what we envision. This is the way we can truly manifest in a fashion that benefits us. When we are truthful about our current state, the old will fall way, and the new will arrive. If you are reading these epiphanies, or any self-improvement resource for that matter, they all require a truthful analysis of the present. Truth is an underlying characteristic of a genuine individual who wishes to change their current circumstances.

"People can't change the truth, but the truth can change people" – Unknown.

Epiphany #28

COMPASSION

R. Simmons said, "Compassion is the ultimate expression of your highest self."

Compassion is the ability to have sympathetic concern for the misfortune of others. I will add that it also entails having a genuine desire to alleviate the suffering of others. You are elevated to a higher level of consciousness when you help another person go beyond their struggle. The intention for this book is to do just that. That is why you are holding it in your hands at this very moment. How often do we look at the suffering of someone and say, "How can I help?" If you believe in the idea of the collective conscious then when one suffers we all suffer. What happens to one is happening to all.

This forward way of thinking puts us in a delicate position to recognize that the choices we make as individuals, in some respect, affect others. Harry Swimmer said, "If everyone would lend a helping hand to those in need, we would take a huge step in living in a more peaceful world." Compassion is the key to humanity. Coming to a realization that there is something greater than our individual selves is part of the equation in changing our world. What are you doing to show compassion toward others? What can you do outside of your daily life to aid the life of another?

I was privileged to teach at an inner-city middle school for 2 years, and help students with disabilities. Teaching was some of the best work I've done in my entire life. Being concerned with the emotional welfare of others is part of being compassionate. It is endearing and spiritually rewarding to help another human being in need. There is a certain sense of continuity that goes along with being a teacher.

In learning how to meditate, I was first taught to be mindful of my breath. As I progressed, I was taught something called loving kindness. This method teaches the individual to go through a series of steps to radiate compassion. First, you send that compassion to yourself. Then, you send compassion to someone you love dearly. After that, you send compassion to a neutral person in your life. This could be a co-worker or someone you see in passing. Finally, you send an equal amount of compassion to a person you are in conflict with, or one that may be perceived as an enemy. This simple, yet profound, exercise has allowed me to come through some of the most difficult of circumstances. I've been able to re-invigorate myself through the act of compassion.

Our personal well-being bank increases when we give compassion to others. You will also find that by practicing compassion toward others, you will begin to receive compassion in return. It will be nice to have the compassion of others when you require it. Even if you master every epiphany in this book, you will still have times of challenge. We are human beings, and part of our journey is to make mistakes, and accept the errors of others. That is what makes the process of life so enriching. Learn from your misfortunes, and your reality will shift. Have compassion for yourself, and others, in whatever situation you may find yourself. Compassion is instrumental in Dream Mechanics. With compassion you can alter the dream for yourself, but also the dream of others. By being compassionate toward one another, we help alleviate the suffering of the entire world. "Until he extends the circle of his compassion to all living things, man will not himself find peace." – Albert Schweitzer.

Epiphany #29

GRATITUDE

Dr. Robert Holden said, "The miracle of gratitude is that it shifts your perception to such an extent that it changes the world you see."

This statement literally sums up your ability to create your reality. No self-improvement book would be complete without discussing the component of gratitude. Gratitude is an appreciation for everything you have at this moment. By appreciating all the awesome things you currently have, a space opens to create even more things to be grateful for. Gratitude is the moving force of Dream Mechanics. I get grateful every single day during my daily meditation. At some point during my meditation, I usually set aside time to express all that I am grateful for. In my mind, I go through a list of all the things I am grateful for. For example, it could be the roof over my head, the blanket that keeps me warm at night, the blood running through my veins, the legs I have to walk with, or even the money in my bank account. I list off various items that I am grateful for one by one, from the small and insignificant things, to the large and important stuff.

I also visualize future things that I am grateful for. It is wise to do this because you put yourself in a state of gratitude before the actual event or thing manifests as your reality. For example, be grateful for the places you are going to visit before you visit them. Be grateful for the health you're going to have even if you're not the healthiest person at the present moment. I guarantee you will get there. If you can visualize where you want to be in your mind, then your physical body will follow, and it will become your reality. If you can program the mind to already believe something exists before it actually happens, then you're using a technique that is extremely powerful.

Most religions teach us to be grateful during prayer or while saying grace. But, they leave out the mechanics for making things reality. We must feel fortunate for all that has been bestowed upon us especially at the present moment. Look around you and see everything that is a blessing in your life and count each one! Gratitude should be palpable. Feel it when you list all the things you are grateful for. Get emotional, cry, get giddy, and shout with joy if you have to, but feel how fortunate you are to have your present situation. If you can genuinely do that, then more blessings will come your way. Praise the people you are surrounded with. Be grateful that they have come into your life. They are there to learn from you, and you are there to learn from them. It is no accident that you are in the situation you find yourself in. The reason you are there, in this moment, is to realize that you brought it into your existence. You've manifested the majority of your life experience. Accept that, and then use the tools in this book to manifest exactly what you prefer in your life. The power is in your hands.

This book is designed to help you get unstuck, and find your way. Gratitude puts you on the path you want to be on, and it opens doors where there were only walls. Cultivating an attitude of gratitude provides the energy for you to manifest, and the stairway to reach a higher level of being. So, what are you grateful for today?!

Epiphany #30

SYNCHRONICITY

Janet Stephenson said, "Synchronicity is not about orchestration – it is allowance of manifestation."

Did you ever get that feeling when things just seem to fall into place? Or, you receive a phone call from someone you've been thinking about. Perhaps you meet with a special someone who seems to come into your life out of nowhere. Maybe it's those moments when things just seem to come together. That can all be described as synchronicity.

Synchronicity is when events occur in your life that do not seem to be related, but in all actuality are very much connected. Why is synchronicity important to Dream Mechanics? Synchronicity is significant because it is a skill to recognize when it is happening. You have to identify what is coming into your life that is relative to your dreams. Knowing how to discern these factors is ideal when creating your reality. If you overlook them, you may miss something that the universe is attempting to deliver to you. Carl Jung described these moments as, "meaningful coincidences." He said, "Synchronicity is an ever present reality for those who have the eyes to see it." Those individuals who are awakened have special eyes to see through the veil of illusion. With synchronicity, we learn to create our reality by allowing our manifestations to take place, and then build upon them. We listen and follow the clues that are being presented to us. Things will just seem to line up as if we pre-designed it for ourselves.

Sometimes synchronicity will happen in the form of an accident to move you away from where you are, and in the direction you should be going. Are there really any coincidences? Think of all the major events that have happened to you over your entire life. Do you believe they were just by chance? Did they just happen or did you unknowingly manifest them? Are coincidences times of contact and connection with an unseen force? These questions are important in understanding the mechanics of the dream. The answers to them correlate to Dream Mechanics. If we look at synchronicity in a manner that has significant meaning, we can be guided toward living some of our wildest dreams. Synchronicity is an indicator that we are getting closer to bringing our dreams into existence, hence intentionally creating the reality we desire. Keeping an open mind when summoning synchronicity is important when certain signs are presented.

I have a quote that I cut out of a magazine which reads, "I am at the right place at the right time." By putting this quote on my bathroom mirror, where I see it every day, the words would embed themselves into my sub-conscious. Unbeknownst to me, I would begin to actually find myself in situations that benefited me. I would continually find myself at the right place at the right time. I could feel it. Everything would just click. A job would present itself when I desired one. Certain people would appear in my life when I required them to. Travel would beckon me when it was appropriate. Money would manifest when needed. These are all areas of synchronicity, and they offer a glimpse into our destiny. You've got to be in-tune with the magic, and you will manifest more for yourself. Think of all the successful people you know. Do you believe that everything happened to them by luck? Some luck maybe, but I believe they all share the same common denominator in their success. They've left room for things to sync. And, they acted when they recognized those moments. When you are properly connected with the universe it gives you signals. Follow them!

Nancy Thayer proclaimed, "The universe is always speaking to us… sending us little messages, causing coincidences and serendipities, reminding us to stop, look around, to believe in something else, something more." Synchronicity can happen in conversation, or at some unexpected moment. Once you are conscious, you will become receptive to the mystery of synchronicity. Pay attention to the messages you receive because they have the ability to help your dreams and reality converge. Recognizing synchronicity in your life can lead to your ultimate reality.

Epiphany #31

CHOICE

Richard Bach indicated, "Every person, all the events of your life, are there because you have drawn them there. What you choose to do with them is up to you."

One of the greatest assets of a human being is our power to choose. Choice is what distinguishes us from every other living being on the planet. When we realize the gift of choice, we can design our reality accordingly.

Ever wonder why some individuals have a certain kind of life experience? Why are some people happy and privileged and others not so much? It all comes down to the choices we make. Choice enables us to evaluate situations, and make conscious decisions that coincide with our dreams. Choice allows us to take alternate routes when necessary. We are not at the mercy of life. Although I am a big proponent of going with the flow, choice is a tool that we can use when combining our reality with the unseen forces. The tricky part is that we must be careful not to heavily interfere with what the universe has in store for us. We can co-create with the universe in a safe and effective manner by making strategic choices that are positive in nature. We do this based upon how we feel. Our intuitive feelings provide us guidance so we can make good choices.

Far too often we give our ability to choose away. It is important that we become aware of the times we sacrifice our gift of choice in our relationships, careers, and personal endeavors. Choosing a path that is in alignment with what we wish to create is dynamic. If a person or situation feels uncomfortable, those are signals from the universe that we must make a new choice, or excuse ourselves from that type of situation. Otherwise, we are granting permission to be a part of the reality that another person may be creating. We become part of someone else's dream rather than understanding the mechanics of the dream as a whole. This is a where we must discern what and who we participate with. We are only as a good as the people and places we surround ourselves with. Accepting that certain situations and persons teach us various lessons is important, but knowing when to separate so we can grow is even more important. Sometimes drastic measures are necessary if you are serious about creating your desired reality.

Keep in mind that making a choice should not be mixed with surrender. Surrendering to life is important at times, and it goes hand in hand with the choices we make. The good thing about the choices we make, even the ones that seem to create challenges, is that we have destiny to fall back on. You see, with the belief in destiny, no choice whether we label them, good or bad, is going to hurt us. All choices are made to place us closer to the ultimate destiny that awaits. Trust your choices even when they appear to be uncertain. Our choices lead to our fate and evolution which determines our life experience. This revolving planet is a dream machine. Think of our choices as the fuel for that machine. The world will be a better place when we start to make better choices collectively. Choices built upon love, peace, trust, and humanity are vital to the health of the whole world. I am grateful for the moment that I realized the power of choice. It moved me to another level of being, and made me a better person. I began to look at how my choices were effecting my reality, and in some sense, the reality of others.

I decided to add this epiphany into the book after the first manuscript was submitted. The reason it was added is because I've met so many individuals on my path who either don't understand they have a choice, or are blinded to its gift. Lack of understating choice is a world-wide epidemic that is holding individuals back from reaching their full potential. Choiceless-ness is plaguing all cultures, and it is time to take back the power to choose. Many people don't realize that they can choose to leave a job that drains them, and choose to do all the things they wish to do. Instead, they will come up with excuses, or stay with the same group of people because it makes them feel normal. It makes them feel safe. Expecting different results when you are doing the same thing over and over again is defined as insanity.

Two instrumental ways to create your desired reality is to choose better circumstances for yourself, and become a positive, independent entity. Separate yourself from the pack you hang around in if they are not supporting your dreams, and reach for more. Or, risk missing out on the amazing adventures that lie ahead. Often times we relinquish our happiness to satisfy others. Co-dependency veers its' unfulfilling head in our conditional relationships. Be careful, and deliberately choose healthy relationships with family, friends, career, and loved ones. Choose happiness in all that you do, otherwise you slowly give your joy away. We have dominion over our happiness. All that surrounds us is a direct result of the choices and decisions we make. Take inventory of your life, and order more of the stuff you like. Our ability to specifically choose the results we wish to see in our life is empowering! The choices we make define and build our character for who we wish to be, and the reality we wish to create. Through choice we are able to learn and expand our knowledge in a variety of capacities. Be conscious of the choices you make for they are the currency of a blissful life experience.

“Everything in your life is a reflection of a choice you have made. If you want different results, start making different choices” – Unknown.

Epiphany #32

INSPIRATION

"Inspiration is around every corner, so go for a walk" – Unknown.

True inspiration can move mountains. When you discover what inspires you, then you have armed yourself with an incredible tool. A person who manifests uses inspiration to create reality just like an artist uses inspiration to create art. Inspiration can come from a variety of sources. It can be harnessed from art, music, nature, books, environment, and other individuals. When we are truly inspired, the world becomes our playground. We become a source for others to strive toward, and appear as an instrument of what is possible.

Those who work with inspiration do not know the meaning of the word - can't. An inspired person is unstoppable. An inspired person reaches for the stars with a feeling of exhilaration, in all they do, because inspiration arouses a feeling of energy when you accomplish something. An inspired person is filled with the urge to do or feel something, especially something creative. There is no cost for inspiration, and it can be obtained by simply breathing. This is monumental! In this sense, just think about the abundance of inspiration that is all around you. We can extract inspiration in meditation, or in some other fashion where we simply focus on our breath. Inspiration pulls you from the depths of being stuck.

Many friends approach me with this challenge. How do I become inspired? How do I fill myself with this ability to do things? I always tell them to inspire themselves. It's so easy, and so necessary in the creation of reality. Get excited for your life. Get energized about gaining the knowledge in this book, and be excited to put it to use. It's all here for you in black and white. This book will lead to others, and it certainly is a foundation to begin the creative process. You will see your life take flight by putting these epiphanies to good use. They will help move you in the direction you wish to go. Using these components to influence your reality is a natural progression.

History says, "Know thyself." What a powerful, yet simple statement. In the spirit of inspiration, it is in knowing yourself that you can accept what is best for you. It is knowing yourself that you understand you create your reality, and you have the wisdom to manifest anything you wish. The moment we realize that happiness and abundance is our birth right, is the moment we begin to thrive because we no longer settle for anything else. You, who is reading this book, are an amazing person! You have the tenacity and knowledge to achieve anything! You are limitless and free! Be what you have always intended to be and let nothing inhibit your aspirations. And when you take a small step in the direction of your dreams, more steps will open up to you. Your life, and all that is in it, is a reflection of you. Your life is your creation, and thus all it entails is a mirror image of your thoughts.

Mike Dooley noted, "Thoughts become things, choose the good ones." We are the designers of our life according to what we think. Our thoughts matter because what we think determines our reality. You can say that your life is as inspiring as you "think" it to be. Fill your mind with astronomical thoughts of inspiration, and your life will soar to phenomenal heights.

Where-ever you have been, and where-ever you are going, are all part of the masterpiece that you are crafting. If the life you lead is one that you are proud to share with others, then you are on the right track. If the life you lead inspires others, you have been fortunate in a variety of ways. Find things that inspire you on a frequent basis, and let that inspiration encapsulate your being. You will bring that sense of joy in all that you do. People will see it, emulate it, and want it for themselves. If you can transfer a feeling to someone that motivates them to do better for themselves, then you have been given one of life's greatest gifts. Inspiring others is truly a wonderful blessing, and a dynamic component of Dream Mechanics. That being said, "Your life is your message to the world, make sure it is inspiring" – Unknown.

Epiphany #33

DESTINY

"Destiny is all about the choices we make and the chances we take" – Unknown.

Destiny can be described as the hidden power that arranges the future. It revolves around the idea that events are predetermined. Some call this fate! What is the power that determines the course of events? Are there any accidents in life? What about coincidence and synchronicity? The power that determines the course of events in our lives are our thoughts. The frequency of our thoughts, when adjusted properly, leads to manifestation. The power of the mind is the designer of our fate. The thoughts that go on in our mind have a direct impact on our life experience. Mind over matter is a real and tangible way to create our reality. When you are in-sync with life, and are going with the flow, things will manifest in ways that will blow you away. When you get so good at aligning your thoughts, you will create a spectacular reality. It will continually surprise you, and take you along many amazing paths. The people you will meet along the way will also be in alignment, and they will come into your life for a purpose. Your life will literally come full circle, and you will have reached your final destination.

Your eyes are open now, and awakening is only the beginning. Now it's time to implement all you have learned. It's time to create your reality. I'm talking about the reality you have always dreamed of. The one that has you living the life of your dreams. Reaching your destiny often requires taking the road less traveled. It means carving your own path when there isn't one. There is a power, or a force that we can tap into to some degree. Once we identify it, we just have to place ourselves on its trajectory, and the rest will take care of itself.

We must monitor what we are doing in our present moment. Look around you. Are you manifesting the things you want in order to live out your destiny? Or, are you just looking at the same walls, and moving through the same routine day in and day out? Break free from your self-imposed prison and you will lead a life of fulfillment, excitement, and enlightenment! Our destiny is determined by taking those leaps of faith, getting out of our comfort zone, and embracing our fears. These are the areas that can keep us from reaching the end zone if we do not address them. They are the barriers we must surpass, or break through, to reach our ultimate destination.

We are all travelers through the jungles of time and space. If you pause and ponder the situation, we are living on a circular planet suspended in space. That planet is rotating and moving on a precise orbit around the sun in a cyclical fashion. Rotating around the earth is another circular shaped rock called the moon. If that's not enough to present to you that there is a geometric pattern to all that exists, then reaching your destiny could be a challenge. Recognize that everything is cyclical…including our lives! Your destiny is waiting to be fulfilled. Get out of your own way, and start to unveil the destiny that awaits you. See the light in this wonderful adventure we call life!

Remember, you cannot force destiny, you can only place your trust in its' mystical flow. When is the last time you took an uncalculated risk? Sometimes, uncovering your destiny comes from taking the road you didn't necessarily want to take. It is on those unchartered paths that one comes face to face with their destiny. Embark on your journey right here and right now. Or if you have already set sail, then carry on in a confident fashion using some of the tools that have been set forth. You are guided, you are cared for, and you deserve to enjoy the ride.

Epiphany #34

LIVING THE DREAM

Living the dream is easier than you think. There is a science to living the dream. If ever there was a book to put that science in a systematic, organized body, then it is this one. Dream Mechanics is a tried and true compilation of ideas that provide you the tools to live the dream! The epiphanies that have been delivered to you in this book have come to me along my journey. These epiphanies are the sparks of a life well lived. I have been blessed to share them with you in this practical guide. Utilize them, and incorporate them in your life. They work! I use them on a daily basis.

Once you start putting these concepts into practice, your reality will change. Absorb them, and allow them to resonate deep within you. Have an un-wavering belief in optimism, and you can create the life of your dreams. You can live the dream right here, right now, on this very earth. You can be a walking, talking dream maker. People often ask me how I stay positive in a world so divided. To them I say, division is a matter of perception. I see the world as a whole with various parts that must work together for peace to emerge. Being conscious of my personal decisions, and careful not to take sides is one way to promote unity. I've been able to see the world as a better place by staying positive, but remaining neutral. I wake up every morning, ready to go, regardless of what the daily news may report. I am eager to start my day because I love what I do, I love life, and I manifest the things I want to see in my reality.

Henry Ford said, "Whether you think you can, or you think you can't, either way you're right." This quote has stayed with me since my journey began. I find it to be so true, and vital to grasp its' meaning. Your thinking determines your reality, so be careful what you think! And, pay attention to what you're putting into your mind on a daily basis. What kind of music are you listening too? What television shows are you watching? What books are you reading? What kind of conversations are you having? Are these conversations about ideas that are uplifting? All of these things matter, and effect the nature of your reality.

It is our responsibility to fill our minds with beautiful, happy images because the images we place in our subconscious will manifest in our lives. Align your thoughts and yourself with situations and people who are at a higher level. Place images in your environment that you will see daily of all the things you wish for. Explore this beautiful planet. See how other people and cultures live. Go beyond your own backyard, and you will receive gifts that you can only imagine. Make a positive contribution to the world in any way that you possibly can.

The idea that we can direct our dreams has been mentioned in many cultural and religious platforms. The Mayans, the Hindus, the Incans, the Toltecs and the list goes on and on. Even Hollywood has made some of the most successful movies about the dream-reality concept. Many individuals in my inner circle often say to me, "You live in a dream world man." My response to them is, you bet I am! And, that dream is filled with adventure, abundance, and bliss. That's the "stuff" that dreams are made of, and that's what materializes in my reality.

The reflection that we see in the mirror every single day speaks volumes. If you are happy with the image staring you back in the face, then you have achieved something that many individuals only dream of. Love yourself, love your life, and love others. It's been a simple formula since time immemorial. The mechanics of the dream have been laid out in this book. Utilize them, and you just might find yourself in the most amazing places, having the most momentous adventure!

I leave you with this final quote from Scottie Somers, "It's not the things that you accumulate in life that people will remember you by; it's the gifts you share with others that leave an everlasting impression."

Wishing you well on your journey...

Song of the Open Road

by

Walt Whitman

Afoot and light-hearted, I take to the open road,
Healthy, free, the world before me,
The long brown path before me, leading wherever I choose.

Henceforth I ask not good-fortune—I myself am good fortune;
Henceforth I whimper no more, postpone no more, need nothing,
Strong and content, I travel the open road…

. . . From this hour, freedom!
From this hour I ordain myself loos'd of limits and imaginary lines,
Going where I list, my own master, total and absolute,
Listening to others, and considering well what they say,
Pausing, searching, receiving, contemplating,
Gently, but with undeniable will, divesting myself of the holds that would hold me . . .

. . . I inhale great draughts of space;
The east and the west are mine, and the north and the south are mine.

I am larger, better than I thought;
I did not know I held so much goodness.

All seems beautiful to me;
I can repeat over to men and women, You have done such good to me,
I would do the same to you.

I will recruit for myself and you as I go;
I will scatter myself among men and women as I go;
I will toss the new gladness and roughness among them;
Whoever denies me, it shall not trouble me;
Whoever accepts me, he or she shall be blessed, and shall bless me.

About the Author

John Moreschi Jr. is a visionary who thrives on living life intentionally! Born in New York City, John is a global citizen and calls many places home. He began his journey of self-discovery by moving to Las Vegas at the age of 19, where he completed a Bachelor of Science Degree in Hospitality Administration. He held various positions with some of the industry's leading companies. John proceeded on a path of enlightenment by completing a Master of Science in Education at St. John's University in New York. He has taught on the middle school and collegiate levels. His quest has taken him around the world to learn and study with an array of teachers, gurus, and cultures. He has visited all 7 Continents, all 50 of the United States, & all 7 Wonders of the New World! John practices meditation and assists in fundraising efforts both here at home and abroad. He considers himself a life-long learner, and a pioneer of the positive thought movement.

Printed in the United States
by Baker & Taylor Publisher Services